LEGENDARY STANLEY CUP STORIES

BRIAN MCFARLANE

LEGENDARY STANLEY CUP STORIES

BRIAN McFARLANE

Fenn Publishing Company Ltd.

Bolton, Ontario

Fenn Publishing Company Ltd.

LEGENDARY STANLEY CUP STORIES
A Fenn Publishing Book / First Published in 2008

Fenn Publishing Company Ltd.
Bolton, Ontario, Canada
www.hbfenn.com

The publisher gratefully acknowledges the support of the Canada Council for the Arts and the Ontario Arts
Council for its publishing program. We acknowledge the support of the Government of Ontario through the
Ontario Media Development Corporation's Ontario Book Initiative.

Mixed Sources
Cert no. SW-COC-001271
© 1996 FSC
FSC

We acknowledge the financial support of the Government of Canada through the Book Publishing Industry
Development Program (BPIDP) for our publishing activities. Care has been taken to trace ownership of copy-
right material in this book and to secure permissions. The publishers will gladly receive any information that
will enable them to rectify errors or omissions.

Text design: Kathryn Zante
Printed and bound in Canada

Library and Archives Canada Cataloguing in Publication

McFarlane, Brian, 1931-
    Legendary Stanley Cup stories / Brian McFarlane.

ISBN 978-1-55168-342-3 (bound).--ISBN 978-1-55168-362-1 (pbk.)

    1. Stanley Cup (Hockey)--History. 2. McFarlane, Brian, 1931-.
3. Stanley Cup (Hockey)--Anecdotes. 4. Sportscasters--Canada--Biography.
I. Title.

GV847.7.M36 2008   796.962'648   C2008-903663-8

There was a phone message for me when I got home. My daughter Brenda, my award-winning-playwright daughter living in San Diego, California, had called:

> "Hi Dad. Those books you sent me—the hockey books. I was eating my cereal this morning when I started reading one of them—*The Best of It Happened in Hockey*. Those stories you write are incredible. And I'm not even interested in hockey! But you sure know how to tell a great story. I got all emotional reading them—all teary-eyed. Can't wait to read your *Legendary Stanley Cup Stories*."

A daughter's kind words can touch an author deeply.
This one's for you, Brenda.

Contents

IV. Expansion Brings New Champs

V. Individual Headline-Makers

Introduction

The Perfect Parting Gift

Thank you, Lord Stanley, for your whimsical gift to hockey. Thanks, too, to your sons Algernon and Arthur, and your daughter, Lady Isobel Stanley, for their involvement in the game as players. Women's hockey owes a great debt to Lady Stanley. All of you hockey-playing Stanleys were true pioneers of the game. You experienced the joy of playing on your own little outdoor rink in Ottawa. You learned the skills of skating and stickhandling and the thrill of scoring goals. Without you Stanleys—without your passion and your influence—well, there never would have been a trophy named the Stanley Cup.

When you reached the end of your term as governor general of Canada (1888–1893), it was kind of you, Lord Stanley, after heeding the pleas of your children and others, to donate a small silver bowl to "the amateur hockey champions of Canada." Too bad you couldn't have lived another hundred years or more. You would have been amazed at all the commotion your gift has caused, the passion and excitement it has created, not to mention the controversies. In time, the Cup trustees permitted professional teams—and American teams—to compete for your trophy. You could never have predicted that your small silver bowl, purchased from Collis and Company in London for approximately $50, would become one of the most avidly sought trophies in the world of sport. Nor could you have conceived that teams would travel thousands of miles, and spend millions of dollars, in desperate efforts to claim it.

How proud you would be, Lord Stanley, if you could see teams from Florida to California, from Montreal to Vancouver, their rosters loaded with multimillionaire players from many nations, battle through several weeks of gruelling playoffs every spring—with millions of avid fans watching on a device we call television and with hundreds of thousands more paying outrageous prices for tickets to the games—just to get their hockey mitts on your coveted gift to the game. I'm sure you would shake your head in disbelief if you knew that teams from Tampa Bay and Raleigh, North Carolina (named after your countryman, Sir Walter Raleigh, the explorer who brought tobacco and potatoes back to England), and a team from far-off Anaheim, California—yes, California, sir—were recent winners of your coveted trophy.

Your original bowl, I might add, has grown considerably since 1893, when you instructed an aide to purchase it for you in England—for what was it?—a mere $50.

We all regret, Lord Stanley, that you were recalled to England before you even saw a Stanley Cup playoff game. But you did encourage your fellow Brits to take up the game. Why, on your return, you even captained a team of Stanleys in a game played on thin ice against members of the Royal family behind Buckingham Palace. And whipped all those dukes and other lords handily.

But, poor chap, you never got to applaud your favourites—the Ottawas—as they triumphed time and time again. You can't possibly know it, sir, but you have the distinction of being the only man inducted into the Hockey Hall of Fame who never witnessed a Stanley Cup playoff game. Never saw a single Cup goal scored.

As Canada's governor general from 1888 to 1893—that means you were the Queen's representative to the Dominion, right?—you and your wife even donned skates from time to time to join your friends and family on a well-maintained sheet of natural ice next to your mansion, Government House in Ottawa. Those must have been fun times, playing shinny with members of your family. Why, two of your sons, Arthur and Algernon, became so skilled they played with a touring hockey team—the Rebels.

Sir, I found a photo in the National Archives of your daughter, Lady Isobel, playing hockey with her friend Lulu Lemoine (what a lovely name) and other ladies on that sheet of ice. Lady Isobel played the game wearing a long white gown. Surely it's the earliest photo ever taken of a female player.

Lord Stanley, you may or may not be pleased to know that the moneyed moguls of a 30-city league in North America—the National Hockey League—now have full control of your gift to "amateur hockey in Canada." But rest assured your trophy has a safe home, where countless fans come to gaze at it—awestruck. They stare in wide-eyed wonder at it, then move on to marvel at its descendant, the "new" Stanley Cup, with more than 2,200 names engraved on its gleaming, elongated surface. You would be proud to know, sir, that your gift to the game is revered throughout the world.

Yes, Lord Stanley, your little bowl, now old and brittle, sits safely in the Hockey Hall of Fame in Toronto. Back in the 1960s, a Montreal silversmith made an exact replica of your handsome gift. The replica sits atop a huge base on which the names of all the champion players are engraved. It looks really smashing, sir. You would be amazed. Your name went on in 1945 as Stanley of Preston, Lord. There are two other Stanleys on the Cup—Allan Stanley and Barney Stanley. I don't imagine they are related to you.

Yours is now the oldest championship trophy among all the team sports—seven years older than the Davis Cup for tennis. The Montreal Canadiens have won your Cup a record 24 times and a lightweight Montreal centreman, Henri Richard, has his name engraved on your Cup a record number of times—11. A former Boston defenceman, sturdy Raymond Bourque competed for it the most number of seasons—21. A slippery sniper named Wayne Gretzky—he might remind you of One-Eyed Frank McGee from your era—holds most of the individual Stanley Cup records, including most goals (122), most assists (260), and most points (382). His friend Mark Messier is close behind in all three categories.

Today's winners are incredibly well compensated for their efforts. If I revealed their salaries, Lord Stanley, you'd be doing "spinaramas" in your grave.

Thankfully, countless fascinating stories have been chronicled about the chase and capture of your gift to hockey. Many of them are in this book, although some of the familiar ones are not—ones that have been told and retold. Like the one about the Montreal players, en route to a victory party, who once placed your Cup on a street corner while a flat tire was being changed—then drove off without it! Another time, on a dare, an Ottawa player drop-kicked your Cup into the Rideau Canal. Come to think of it, you may find some of the tales to be disrespectful of the Cup, but celebrating players, in their joyous enthusiasm, do get carried away at times, a bit reckless perhaps. Boys will be boys and all that. I hope you understand.

I'm sure you'd find most of the Cup stories I've collected enjoyable, perhaps even fascinating.

There are so many stories.

There was the time a rink manager in Ottawa flooded the ice with two inches of water before a Stanley Cup match, even though, because of a warm spell, there was no hope of the water freezing. He figured it would slow down the visiting team from Kenora—and it did.

Or the time when King Clancy played every position on a team—including goaltender! The time a referee quit and went home, right in the middle of a Stanley Cup game; there's one about a manager who put two goalies in the net; another about a Montreal team that hired a special train to get a star player to a game in Ottawa on time. The player, employed by some firm, couldn't leave until his workday ended. How about the time Chummy Hill scored a playoff goal in Winnipeg— with half a puck!

So many stories, Lord Stanley.

If you knew the full history of your famous Cup, surely you'd say, "By Jove, that little bowl I presented has been involved in some astonishing escapades. I never dreamed it would become so important, so precious, so coveted by so many people."

It really has, Lord Stanley. It really has.

Speaking for hockey fans everywhere, I thank you.

Brian McFarlane

I. Turn-of-the-Century Cup Challenges

Early Interest in the Cup

Even before the first game was played for the Stanley Cup, controversy was common in hockey. Let's look back to 1893, before there were any names scratched on the silver chalice, when spectators were asked to shell out a dollar for prime seats to witness games between Ottawa, Montreal (with three teams), and Quebec. Fans not only complained about the exorbitant ticket prices but grumbled even louder when games did not start on time. Teams were often tardy in arriving at the rink, and spectators were in a surly mood after standing around for an hour or two in drafty, unheated arenas, blowing on their fingers and stamping their feet, wondering if the damn game would ever get underway, wondering if they'd be sleeping on the job the following day.

Newspaper reporters were equally frustrated. They had deadlines to meet, and late-starting games put pressure on them to write their stories in time. What's more, the standing-room positions made available to them were at rinkside, but in the poorest locations. As one of them wrote, "By standing on my tip toes and craning my neck every which way, the pleasure of an occasional glimpse of the play was afforded." Press boxes were still years away.

At the Rideau Rink in Ottawa, fans complained of the incredible din that filled the building all too frequently and worried that hearing loss might result from all the bellowing, booing, and cheering that came from 5,000 throats. Not to mention the cowbells and other noisemakers fans brought to the games.

There was a governing body for hockey back then: the Amateur Hockey Association of Canada. It had been formed as far back as 1886. The senior league schedule, with each club playing eight games, opened on January 7, 1893. The Montreal AAA team finished with a 7–1 mark to claim the championship. The most humiliating loss was suffered by Quebec in the final game of the season. Goalie Frank Stocking gave up all 14 goals in a 14–0 loss to Ottawa. You might say Ottawa "knocked Stocking's socks off."

The Stanley Cup had arrived from England and had been delivered to Rideau Hall, the governor general's mansion in Ottawa. With no fanfare and no playoff series, the small bowl was awarded to the Montreal AAA club as first champions.

But the Montreal players sneered at the freshly bought trophy. "Take it back to Ottawa," they said. "We don't want it."

One would think the team would be proud to claim the title of first Stanley Cup champions. But no. It seems there was friction for some long-forgotten reason between the Montreal Amateur Athletic Association (MAAA) and its affiliated hockey team.

As a result, when Lord Stanley's representatives, the Cup trustees, showed up in Montreal to present the Cup, offering it to the president of the Association, the players on the team were offended. "Let the Association have it. We don't care what you do with it," they muttered.

"But Lord Stanley will be insulted if you refuse it," they were told. "Please reconsider. Hopefully, this idea of a Cup presentation will become an annual event. You'll spoil it if you treat the Cup as a meaningless silver bowl."

The players huddled and decided there might be merit in what the Cup trustees had said. They decided to accept Lord Stanley's gift to hockey, but only if the Cup was taken from the hands of the Association president and awarded to the manager of the hockey team. The trustees promptly complied with the request.

The first bona fide playoff games for the Cup didn't take place until the following year—1894. After four teams finished in a first place tie—all with records of 53—officials of the four teams battled long and hard to determine which would enjoy home-ice advantage. The Quebec representative finally threw up his arms in disgust. "That's it," he said. "I'm withdrawing my team from the playoffs. See you next season."

With three teams remaining, the decision makers, probably by drawing straws, agreed that Montreal AAA would meet Montreal Vics in a playoff game, with the winner to take on Ottawa, which was given a bye.

After Billy Barlow scored twice for the AAA club in a 3–2 win on St. Patrick's Day to eliminate the Vics, the Montrealers went on to defeat Ottawa by a 3–1 score. Barlow was again at his best, scoring twice. Even Harvey Pulford, one of the great defensive stars of the day, couldn't stop the diminutive Barlow. With four goals in two games, Barlow became the first Stanley Cup scoring hero.

And when the Stanley Cup was placed in the hands of the champions, real interest was shown in the presentation.

It wasn't long before a number of clubs from various leagues began demanding a crack at the Cup. For some teams, capturing the Cup became an obsession. It was a challenge trophy, after all, and teams from as far away as Nova Scotia and Manitoba wanted it.

But even then, as new and polished as it was, the Cup was hardly a thing of beauty.

On March 23, 1906, the *Toronto Star* printed the following about the Stanley Cup on the day it was being shipped from Ottawa to Montreal for presentation to the new champions, the Montreal Wanderers:

> The Stanley Cup is not much to look at. The old basin
> has hardly a square inch of blank space on its sides,
> bottom or interior. During its long sojourn in Ottawa
> it has been handled by so many well-known people,
> who took the opportunity of scratching their names on

some portion of the historic bowl.

On examination, one of the first names carved on the interior is that of the late James McGee, the celebrated rugby player. On another portion is that of Mr. Dennis Murphy, M.P. The name of Ottawa alderman Sam Rosenthal occupies a conspicuous place along the rim. Leave it to a pair of politicians to scrawl their names on it. On the outside in small characters, right under the spot where the Rat Portage game is recorded, appears the following: Thomas Stanley Westwick, Feb. 23, '05. While but one year old (What's this? A baby's name on the Cup?), this prospective rover may see the day when he himself, following in the footsteps of his pater, may be one of the challengers or defenders of the trophy.

Other names include P.D. Ross (Cup trustee), Geo. Barnett, Miss Lily Murphy, Ottawa Social Club, (first woman's name on the trophy) and a hundred others.

The original inscriptions on the Cup are known to only those who have inspected it closely. On one side appears "Dominion Hockey Challenge Cup". On the reverse side is the name of the donor around his crest. It reads: "From Stanley of Preston."

The Cup is not worth much in intrinsic value, being only plated, but in hockey lore it is priceless. When the Wanderers and their friends inspect it, there will probably be some chagrin at the diminutive appearance, and numerous inscriptions that deface it.

It is probable in a couple of years a new pedestal will have to be added on account of the congestion of shields which appear on the present one.

In 2007, *Ottawa Sun* columnist Pat MacAdam was visiting Rideau Hall for some reason, and when talk centred on the Ottawa Senators' bid for the Stanley Cup, a cook said, "Ha! We have one just like it in the kitchen."

MacAdam asked for a look and discovered there was indeed a silver bowl in the kitchen that looked exactly like the original Stanley Cup. He lifted it up and found the year 1893 engraved on the base.

"Hmm," he mused. "Perhaps there were two Stanley Cups shipped to Canada."

"What do you use this cup for?" he asked the chef.

"It hold a lotta rice," was the answer.

Winnipeg and Montreal Engage in Memorable Matches

In the late 1890s, there was great enthusiasm for Stanley Cup matches in Canada, especially east of Winnipeg.

In 1896, when the Winnipeg Victorias journeyed to Montreal for a one-game Valentine's Day battle for the Stanley Cup, sportswriters of the era covered the championship from every perspective and filled a multitude of columns that were avidly read by a hockey-hungry populace. Correspondents wrote hundreds—no, thousands—of words about the match, describing everything from the visitors' bright scarlet uniforms to goaltender Whitey Merritt's white cricket pads, as novel then as Jacques Plante's face mask became in 1959.

Such was the interest that the hockey write-ups were splashed over the front pages of the papers, not hidden somewhere inside.

Here are some comments on the thrilling game between the Winnipeg Vics and the Montreal Vics, taken from the *Winnipeg Free Press* following Winnipeg's sensational 2–0 shutout.

> There's joy in the ranks of the Winnipeg touring hockey
> contingent tonight. The magnificent Stanley Cup, emblem-
> atic of the championship of the Dominion, is theirs.
>
> Well and worthy was the victory, long and determined

the battle and for the first time in the history of the champions of the effete east, the Montrealers had to submit to a complete whitewashing.

While recognizing that their pet hockey team was to be confronted by a worthy foe, the eastern champions were all along quite confident that the Winnipeggers would return to the land from which they came—without the trophy. Alas, for the frailty of human hopes Montreal tonight is clothed in sackcloth and ashes and the sports have gone to sleepless beds and with empty pocketbooks. The Peg contingent, on the other hand, has enough money to start a private bank. No less than 2,000 cold "plunkers" were passed over the Windsor Hotel counters tonight and into the jeans of the Winnipeg supporters.

There follows a long description of the game itself and an account of the second goal by the visitors.

The Winnipeg shouts went up from a dozen different portions of the rink where little knots of westerners had secured places of advantage. Every man on the Peg forward line was working like a Trojan. Armytage made one of his oldtime rushes up the side, evading the Montreal defenceman, and a lively scrimmage took place around the Montreal goal. Campbell managed to entice the disc past the Montreal goalkeeper and there was jubilation again in the ranks of the Winnipeg contingent. They surmised rightly that the victory was already theirs. No more goals were taken by either side.

After the match the Winnipegs were entertained to a pleasant supper by the officers of the vanquished club and the best of feeling prevailed.

Meanwhile, a reporter back in Winnipeg filed this description of the reaction of hometown fans.

> It is seldom that Winnipeg has had many evenings of rejoicing in manly sporting circles to equal last night. Everyone was interested in the success of the hockey team in the east and by eight o'clock hundreds of persons had gathered in the city hotels—the Manitoba, the Queens and the Clarendon—to listen to the returns as received by CPR wires from Montreal, while the telephone at the *Free Press* was never idle in response to the requests of the anxious enquirers.
>
> While Winnipeg waited anxiously for the results, the minutes hung very heavily upon the minds of all present. Ten minutes went by and no result. The operator was reminded that several hundred people were waiting. Then Manager Tate announced that Higgy [Higginbottom, a Winnipeg star] had broken his suspenders and a delay was necessary in order for Higgy to secure a new pair.

Back in Montreal, possibly while the suspender hunt was underway, his eastern counterpart was scribbling on a note pad.

> The referee was strictly impartial. He would never argue a case. His word was law. In the east, if a man plays offside he is warned by the referee. If he continues this practice, he is laid off five minutes.
>
> There were about 2,000 persons at the rink who had paid and the Winnipeg club's share will amount to about $160, a rather small percent. But the visitors are so anxious to win the Cup, they don't care if they never get a cent. Some two dollars has been deducted from the full

amount to pay for a few reserved seats Mr. Howard secured for his mother.

The boards surrounding the rink were extremely low and the puck was often shot or deflected into the crowd, there being no protection for the spectators. The puck was promptly thrown back on the ice by someone in the crowd and the game re-commenced without a faceoff.

Campbell saw a chance and came in from the outside and shot it through the posts [there were no goal nets in those days], striking a spectator with such force behind the goal that he collapsed on his knees like a flash.

The caretaker of the rink was so worked up over the defeat that he cried enough tears to almost fill the big trophy.

When the Victorias returned to Winnipeg a few days later, the hometown reporter wrote:

A right royal welcome was extended to the Winnipeg Hockey team on their return from Montreal, where they gained glory for themselves and fame for the province. Long before the train from the east was due a steady stream of citizens assembled at the CPR depot. When the inevitable "Here She Comes" started it ran through a crowd of several thousand people who swarmed the platform. When the iron horse made its appearance a Union Jack was fluttering in front of its headlight and the cowcatcher was adorned with hockey sticks and brooms, emblematic of the clean sweep in Montreal. The engineer showed the pride he took in his human load by wearing a large piece of Winnipeg colours.

As the train slid to a stop, all eyes were turned to the rear sleeper from which the champions emerged, to be taken in charge by their enthusiastic friends. Captain Armytage led the procession and behind him came Messrs. Flett, Higginbottom, Bain, Campbell and Howard. Mr. Merritt, the crack goalkeeper, who arrived on an earlier train, was there to hand them high gray hats adorned with the club colours, which gave the champions a truly distinguished appearance. To the tune of "See the Conquering Heroes Come," played by the Dragoon Band, which kindly lent its services to make the welcome a worthy one, the conquering heroes were escorted to the rear of the depot where Mr. Jordon had cabs at their disposal. The players and officers filled five cabs which, headed by the band, moved upon Main Street. A great many other rigs got in line and hundreds of citizens followed on foot. The Stanley Cup trophy, coveted by every hockey team in the Dominion, occupied a prominent place in the leading cab and was the center of admiring eyes of those who lined the street.

At the hotel, another immense crowd had gathered, and when Mayor Johnston rose to speak, he was greeted by the shouts of several thousand proud citizens. He spoke of the good to be derived from the pursuit of manly and healthful sports and expressed the hope that the peerless seven would long be spared to defend the title they so nobly won.

Then there were loud calls for Mr. Armytage who upon rising was greeted with great cheers. The worthy captain took but a few minutes to thank his large audience for their enthusiastic welcome and stated that he hoped the Stanley Cup would long remain a prominent feature in the city of Winnipeg.

At the conclusion of the speech-making, the team and the ubiquitous newspapermen adjourned to the smoking room where the capacious trophy was filled to the brim with Champagne.

Many were the trophies and souvenirs exhibited by the boys, pieces of ribbon worn on the memorable occasion being eagerly sought after by enthusiastic friends. Chief interest centered on the game puck, which has been embellished almost out of recognition. On the face of it is a silver shield with the names Whitey, Higgy, Army, Roddy, Haddy, Tote and Dan. On the reverse side is a similar shield, surmounted with the figure of a charging Buffalo, with the inscription: Montreal, February 14, 1896. Score 2–0.

Three seasons later, during the final year of the century, the Winnipeg Vics were on another Cup hunt, and again, they faced the Montreal Vics— on eastern ice.

In game one, Montreal scored twice in the final minute to eke out a 2–1 victory.

Game two was just as close. With Montreal leading 3–2, Bob McDougall of Montreal slashed Winnipeg's Tony Gingras across the legs. Gingras lay writhing on the ice until his teammates picked him up and carried him to the dressing room.

Referee Jim Findlay sent McDougall to the box for two minutes.

"Two minutes!" screamed the Winnipeggers. "McDougall should get a life suspension."

"Two minutes," repeated Findlay.

The visitors surrounded Findlay, demanding that he change his call. They shouted and screamed and jostled him.

"You should see the gash on Gingras's leg," one of them said. "Then you'll change your mind."

"All right, I'll take a look," Findlay volunteered.

He went to the dressing room and examined Gingras. It was confirmed.

The player had suffered a deep gash on his leg.

"But I won't change my mind," Findlay ruled. "It's still two minutes. And since you don't care for my refereeing, I'm through officiating this game. I'm going home, gentlemen."

He took off his skates, hailed a horse drawn cab, and went home.

Officials chased after him and pleaded with him to come back. Eight thousand people in the stands wanted to see their beloved Montrealers win the Cup. And there was no other referee available, although you'd think someone in the crowd would have volunteered to replace Findlay.

Finally, the referee agreed to return. But when he did, the stands were less than half full and the Winnipeg team had scattered. He gave the few that remained an ultimatum.

"On the ice in 15 minutes—or else!"

They ignored him. After 15 minutes, Findlay shrugged and awarded the unfinished Stanley Cup game to Montreal.

When the Vics Met the Wellingtons

One of my all-time favourite Stanley Cup stories goes way back—to 1902 and a best-of-three series between the Winnipeg Vics and the Toronto Wellingtons. Front-page stuff. Fans came from miles around to jam into the 3,000-seat arena to witness the first Stanley Cup matches played in Manitoba. Some young men from Saskatchewan paid the exorbitant sum of $15 per ticket. A party of 20 from Minnesota had never seen a hockey match and were dismayed to find that all the seats had been sold. They were allowed to sit in the ladies' waiting room, where they watched the game through the windows.

The Winnipeg Vics skated onto the ice for the warmup wearing long, gold dressing gowns over their uniforms. The referee, a Mr. McFarlane, had a little chat with both teams prior to dropping the puck. While he talked, snow fell through cracks in the roof and formed lines on the ice.

Midway through the first game, one of the "lifters"—a player noted for his ability to hoist the puck down the ice—lifted it high over the players' heads. But it did not come down! It was lodged among the rink rafters. The players milled about and hurled their sticks upwards while the spectators laughed and cheered. The player whose stick finally dislodged the puck received a standing ovation.

There was another long delay when a Newfoundland dog jumped on the ice and a merry chase resulted.

A reporter wrote of a most unusual goal: "In a scrimmage near the Vic's goal, the puck was broken cleanly in two. Toronto's 'Chummy' Hill grabbed one piece and sailed in on Brown, shooting the goal. Brown said afterwards he thought the play had stopped with the breaking of the puck and was taken by surprise. Referee McFarlane was forced to make a quick decision and he allowed the goal to stand."

It remains the only Stanley Cup series in history in which a goal was scored with half a puck.

A recurring phrase in a newspaper account of the game catches the eye: "Gingras was sent to the fence by Mr. McFarlane." Later in the summary, it appears again. "Gingras was told once again to sit on the fence." Finally, it becomes obvious. There was no penalty box for naughty Gingras to sit in. Penalty boxes hadn't been invented yet. Gingras simply sat on the low boards surrounding the rink until the referee told him he could play again.

There was another playoff "first" when the puck sailed over the boards into the crowd. Normally, the spectator catching the puck would return it promptly to the ice and play would continue. But the fan broke with tradition by pocketing the puck. Despite pleas from players, officials, and other spectators, he refused to give up his souvenir. Finally, another puck was sent for and the game continued.

One reporter wrote about the play of the Wellington's McKay: "McKay tried to do too much work and killed himself. In the first half he was the life of the team but several hard body checks put him out of business and he had to retire. He came on again after a rest, but could not stand the pace and fell on the ice. He had to be removed to the dressing room."

Winnipeg won the series in two straight games and entertained the Wellingtons at a reception following the victory. The Stanley Cup was fetched from a jewellery store window, where it had been on display, and presented to the winners.

The Winnipeg papers on the following day were filled with lengthy descriptions of the play and quotes from the men involved. The Cup victory was front-page news, the game coverage eye-popping. Neat little pen-and-ink illustrations of the game highlights and the players involved, including one of Gingras of the Vics sitting on the fence, were prominent in the multi-page coverage.

Back home in Toronto, one of the Wellingtons cried when he heard about all the excitement he had missed. His parents had refused to let him go on the trip to Winnipeg, stating he was far too young for such gallivanting.

Toronto fans followed the course of the series in an unusual manner. They opened windows or stood outside in order to hear a blast of the whistle from the Toronto Railway Company. A reporter in Winnipeg would phone the Toronto *Globe* with the game result. A man on duty there would call the railway company. If Winnipeg won, there would be two blasts on the whistle, which could be heard throughout the city. If Toronto won, three blasts would signal the victory. Alas, after each game, a third blast was never heard. Fans went back indoors, windows were slammed shut. They could only imagine how the fans in Winnipeg were celebrating their Cup victory.

Albert "The Kid" Forrest Goes for the Cup

At age 17, Albert Forrest was not only the youngest goalie to compete for the Stanley Cup, but he played for the weakest playoff team in Cup history. What's more, he travelled the longest distance to realize his dream of playing for the coveted trophy.

Albert's story borders on the unbelievable.

In 1904, during the latter stages of the great gold rush in the Yukon Territory in northern Canada, young Forrest, whose family was originally from Trois-Rivières, Quebec, was the netminder on a hockey team in Dawson City. Wealthy gold miners had built an indoor arena in the boomtown, and Captain Joe Boyle, an entrepreneur and promoter of prizefights, thought that Forrest and half a dozen of his teammates might be talented enough to win the Stanley Cup. Boldly, he entered a challenge, and to his amazement, the Cup trustees accepted it.

Boyle was a fascinating character. Originally from Woodstock, Ontario, he earned the name "Captain" for his ability to transport hundreds of prospectors to Dawson City over the perilous rapids of the Whitehorse River. While the newcomers sought riches from mining claims, Boyle had a bigger vision. He persuaded the government to lease him 40 acres of prime land. Soon, he was operating a lumber mill, a power company, and a number of other profitable companies. He became known as the "King of the Klondike," and years later books would be written about his colourful life, which included a romance with Marie, the Queen of Romania.

"I'll put up the money for the trip to Ottawa," he promised the Dawson hockey players. "Let's go win the Cup."

The epic story of the trip the Dawson City lads, now nicknamed the "Nuggets," embarked upon had everything but a happy ending. The Nuggets left Dawson City on December 19, 1904, some of them walking, the others on bicycles. When the bicycles broke down in the deep snow, the players hitched rides on passing dogsleds. In time, they arrived in Whitehorse, 350 miles west of their starting point.

That was just the beginning of their trek.

From Whitehorse, they travelled by narrow-gauge railway to Skagway, on the coast of Alaska, where they planned to book passage on a steamship sailing to Vancouver. But they arrived several hours late, and the ship had already departed.

After they waited for five days, another ship arrived, a tramp steamer, and they wearily climbed aboard. But this ship's destination was Seattle, Washington, not Vancouver.

No matter. They landed in Seattle and promptly boarded a train headed north to Vancouver. From Vancouver, another train carried them across the nation to Ottawa. At every stop, they were cheered on by fans who were anxious to see them end the Cup reign of the Ottawa Silver Seven, those "arrogant Easterners."

The Nuggets climbed down from the train on January 12, 1905, after covering close to 4,000 miles in 24 days. Fatigued and lacking condition, they pleaded for a postponement of the best-of-three Cup series.

"Let us get our skating legs back," they asked.

"No way," declared the Ottawa management. "The ice time has been booked, the tickets sold. We'll play tomorrow night."

Ottawa whipped the challengers handily by scores of 9–2 and 23–2.

The latter score remains the most one-sided result in Stanley Cup history. In that match, Ottawa star One-Eyed Frank McGee scored a record 14 goals against young Forrest.

Not only was Forrest the youngest goalie ever to play for the Cup, but he'll be forever listed as the goalie with the worst goals-against record in Cup history.

Poor kid.

But he may have found solace in the Ottawa newspapers. One reporter wrote: "Forrest in goal is a sensation and nothing too complimentary can be said about his work." Another said of him: "Forrest was indeed a marvel. But for him, the score in the series would have been double what it was. Two Ottawa goals were scored when the Yukon's clever young goal-keeper was off the ice [whatever that means], and three others were scored despite off-sides, there being a good yard or two in the one case and a foot in the others."

Fans stayed to the finish in the second game because they wanted to see a world record set for goals in one game. A reporter wrote: "Dawson never had a chance. It was like putting a sugar bun in the hands of a small boy."

Your author has researched this story thoroughly and even discussed Albert's career with some of his descendents. Some questions I had could not be answered. Why, for example, if Forrest was a "sensation" and a "marvel" in the eyes of Ottawans, did he not make a bigger name for himself in hockey with some other team? And how did the teenager talk his parents into letting him embark on such an expedition, one that appeared to be foolhardy and somewhat dangerous, in the first place?

After his Cup appearance, Albert Forrest returned to the Yukon, walking the final 350 miles from Whitehorse to Dawson City. When he finally arrived home, he received a hero's welcome.

The following poem could have been written by Albert Forrest:

Yes, I'm the boy who stood in goal,
Facing pucks he hurled at me.
Yes, I'm the lad whose job it was
To stop the Great McGee.

I tried my best but failed the test,
For the record shows that he
Scored 14 goals in a single game,
And all of them on me.

Oh dear, oh my, it was a catastrophe!

They cheered him loud, they cheered him long.
It was quite a sight to see.
Each time he scored, the more they roared,
"You're our hero, Frank McGee."

I stood there shaken, looking on,
The victim of his spree.
Oh yes, he scored those 14 goals,
It was easy as could be.

I wish he'd done it somewhere else,
And on someone else—not me!
When he tired, his mates took up the slack
Till the score reached 23.

Oh dear, oh my, it was a catastrophe!

Someday, when I'm old and grey
With my grandson on my knee,
I'll tell him of the night I faced
The mighty Frank McGee.

I'll tell him of his blazing shot
And his boundless energy
And how he played with one bad eye—

Why, the man could hardly see!

But his scoring touch was a gift from God,
At least, that's my philosophy.
I'll talk about Lord Stanley's Cup
And how it slipped away from me
Because of hockey's greatest star,
Old One-Eyed Frank McGee.

Oh dear, oh my, it was such a catastrophe!

A few weeks after the whipping administered to Dawson City, an even smaller town took a run at the Stanley Cup. Rat Portage (later to be named Kenora) in northwestern Ontario imported some hockey stars and, along with homegrown talent, iced a splendid hockey team—the Thistles. The Thistles' challenge for the Stanley Cup was accepted and games against Ottawa—the defending Cup holders—were scheduled for March of 1905.

A tremendous crowd of local supporters lined up at the railroad station in Rat Portage on March 3 to bid the Thistles Godspeed and good luck as they departed for the nation's capital. The train pulled out of the station amidst much cheering and rooting. Hundreds of fans bellowed out the war cry of the team:

Red, red, red.
White, white, white
Rat Portage Thistles
Are right, right, right!

In Ottawa, the fans were still smirking over a lopsided lacing of the Dawson City Nuggets. Could tiny Rat Portage be any better than the Klondikers? It didn't seem likely to the fans in the capital.

But they were. Team captain Tom Phillips was a whirlwind on skates in the opening game, scoring five times and leading the westerners to a 9–3 upset. The Thistles wore new McCullough tube skates with thin blades, which gave them an edge in speed and dexterity.

Taunted by their fans, the Ottawa boys resorted to roughhouse tactics in the second game. Every one of the visiting players—only two of whom weighed more than 150 pounds— was on the receiving end of body slams, butt ends, cross checks, and slashes. The referee, Mr. Grant, donned a hard hat to avoid injury and was roasted by the crowd.

Ottawa fans wouldn't have been surprised if the Rat Portage manager had placed two goaltenders in the net. He had tried it before, and the strategy made scoring slightly more difficult for the opposing snipers. There was no rule against the ploy in hockey's early days.

Late in the contest, with Ottawa in front by a 4–2 score, Billy McGimsie of the visitors collapsed in front of his team's goal and lay prone on the ice for some time. The referee gave him a five-minute penalty for obstructing the goal line.

McGimsie went to the box soaked to the skin because there was more than an inch of water covering the natural ice surface. In fact, following the game, Rat Portage officials accused the arena manager of needlessly flooding the ice with plenty of water "in order to slow our boys down."

"It was a dirty Ottawa trick," said the Rat Portage manager. "Water doesn't freeze when it's forty degrees outside. They knew our skates would dig into the soft ice more easily than theirs."

When Ottawa captured the third game of the series by a 5–4 score to retain the Cup, a reporter wrote:

> The Stanley Cup, emblematic of the championship of the world, will remain in Ottawa for another season. In what doubtless was the best and most keenly contested hockey game ever seen here, the Ottawa team last night defeated the challengers 5–4. It was the game of a lifetime. Three times the challenging Thistles were in the lead and 91 seconds before time was up the score was tied.
>
> Then, with only a minute and a half to play, [Harvey]

Pulford and [Frank] McGee took the puck and after some fast combination work landed it between the legs of Thistle goaltender [Eddie] Geroux.

Then what a scene! The 4,000 spectators who thronged the rink simply went wild. Never had such an outburst of enthusiasm followed a goal. Men swarmed on the ice and hugged the victors. It was with difficulty that the ice was cleared for the remaining half minute of play.

Another reporter, from the *Toronto Star*, offered this account of the game:

In the first half there was a judge of play, a sort of second referee. The two officials did not divide their duties as Mr. Davidson often called offsides as well as rough play. His presence on the ice had a good moral influence and kept Ottawa under restraint. In the second half they made up for it, however, and hacked and jabbed their opponents until they were sights to behold. Smith and Moore laid their men out when necessary. Mr. Grant allowed everything to go. Even the Ottawa and Montreal newspapermen were left gasping at his decisions. When Rat Portage seemed sure to score several times he blew his whistle for offsides. The Ottawa players were seen cross checking and jabbing their opponents in the face.

The Thistles returned home battered and bruised. They were angry at Mr. Grant's officiating and the flooding of the ice. But they were also thrilled to have played for the Stanley Cup. And they were determined to regroup and plan their next challenge.

The Great McGee

I would loved to have met the great Frank McGee, the Wayne Gretzky or Sidney Crosby of his era.

The only player to score 14 goals in a Stanley Cup game was Ottawa's blond McGee, one of the greatest scorers to ever grip a hockey stick or lace on a pair of skates. He weighed all of 140 pounds—if that—but he was a whippet on the ice, a wonder.

More than a century has passed since he played for the Ottawa Silver Seven. They said he was the stuff of legends, and they were right. We still write of McGee's exploits today. Aware that sportswriters of the day wrote reams of copy about McGee, I culled old newspaper accounts of his Gretzky-like performances and the following, written by some long forgotten sportswriter, is a testament to his greatness:

> I followed McGee's playing career and every match was the same. Away from home, for example, in a furious Stanley Cup series with the Montreal Wanderers, with about 6,000 people all howling "Get McGee!" I saw Frank knocked cold half a dozen times in the one match and honest, he survived to score the last two goals that won the game. No

one could slow him up. My, but he was game! Taking the puck and beginning a series of slashing attacks, he finally sailed right into the mouth of the net with two defenders doing their best to eat him alive. He took a dozen nasty cracks and still scored one minute before time. Seconds later, he repeated the feat and was able to skate off smiling.

In the dressing room, when he doffed his clothes, he was simply cut all up but he was game. That's why the Ottawa fans loved him, idolized him.

There was another write-up:

How McGee came to the rescue of the Ottawa Hockey Club in 1905, how he played despite the loss of sight in one eye caused by a lifted puck in Hawkesbury one night, how he paced the Stanley Cup in the never to be forgotten series against Kenora, how he brought defeat to the Winnipeg Rowing Club, how he scored 14 goals or more in a single game against Dawson City, how he became the sensation of hockey, his feats at fullback with the old Rough Rider football club—of these facts Frank's friends and admirers could talk on forever. No player of the present day can approach his brilliance. He will never be surpassed.

Billy Grant, sporting editor of the Calgary *News-Telegram*, once graphically described his first impressions of McGee:

They escorted me into an ice-cold rink and I wondered how people could stand the chill. Then someone cleared an aisle near me and I heard a strange clatter of steel as the Ottawa players clambered down the steps from their dressing room. The voices began to hum. Then a wild roar of applause and thousands of excited voices wildly shouting "McGee! McGee! McGee!" I looked around for a big, rugged, broad-shouldered athlete, one who would gaze around theatrically and acknowledge the spontaneous roar of applause that greeted him. I asked a man, "Which one is McGee?" and drew in my breath when he pointed to a fair-haired, blue-eyed stripling who came down last. His hair was perfectly parted, as though he had just stepped out of a tonsorial parlour. His spotless white pants were creased to a knife-like edge, his boots had been polished. For a minute or so I stood spellbound. Then someone formally introduced us and McGee quickly pulled off his gauntlet and held out a soft but muscular hand. Then he jumped over the rail amidst another wild whoop of delight.

He seized the puck at center ice, skated in with the speed of a prairie cyclone and shot. I saw him backcheck furiously, dodge here and there, flash from side to side, stickhandle his way through a knot of struggling players, slap the puck into the open net and go down in a heap as he did so. Then I ceased to wonder why this boyish, doll-like hockey star was the idol of the crowd. I too joined in the hysterical shouting for Frank McGee, the world's greatest hockey player.

During his brief career, McGee played in only 23 regular-season games, but he averaged three goals per game. In the same time frame, he played in 11 Stanley Cup series, in which he scored an incredible 63 goals in 22 games. Again, just shy of three goals per game.

Despite the handicap of being blind in one eye, McGee served overseas in the First World War. He was killed on September 16, 1916, during the great offensive on the Somme.

From one Ottawa newspaper:

> None of Ottawa's losses in the war will be more deeply regretted than that entailed in the death of Frank McGee who endeared himself to the sporting public as a member of the famous old Ottawa hockey team, the Silver Seven. McGee played center for the Stanley Cup holders at the height of their fame and was conceded to be one of the most brilliant and effective players who ever filled that position.

And from another:

> Canadians who knew the sterling stuff of which Frank McGee was made were not surprised when he donned another and new kind of uniform and jumped into the greater and grimmer game of war. Just as in his sporting career he was always to be found in the thickest of the fray. There is no doubt that on the field of battle, Lieut. McGee knew no fear nor shunned any danger. The sympathy of his thousands of admirers will be extended to his family, which has suffered the loss of two (his brother Charles was killed a year earlier) noble members in the great struggle in France.
>
> McGee was 35.
>
> With the death of McGee, there passed one whose athletic fame will always be talked of, and one whose memory will never fade.

A Stanley Cup Battle in 1906

What was the typical Stanley Cup game like over a hundred years ago? In the gaslight era, there were no mammoth arenas, no radio broadcasts of the games, no artificial ice. Players were small—many the size of jockeys. Sticks were shorter. Only the puck was the same.

Teams of seven players and a couple of subs, with no backup goaltenders, played two 30-minute halves. In March, ice conditions could be atrocious—with an inch or two of water slowing play to a crawl. Goal judges were selected from the crowd. They paid for their tickets, found their seats—and surprise! The referee singled them out, directed them to stand behind each goal, and ordered them to wave a handkerchief in the air if the puck crossed the goal line. If they didn't pay attention, or were afraid of being bowled over by incoming forwards, they could be replaced—and often were.

Goaltenders wore cricket pads and unpadded gloves, and a thick glove thrust inside their pants served as a jock. If they fell to the ice, they could be penalized. Each team had a "lifter," a defensive player who, when pressured, lofted the puck down the ice and out of danger.

But let's read an account of a final match for the Stanley Cup—one in 1906 between the famous Ottawa Silver Seven and their archrivals from Montreal, the Wanderers. It's the second game of a two-game series, with total goals to count. The Ottawa cause is hopeless. Or is it? The sportswriter's prose of a century ago fills many columns in his paper because interest in this Cup series is at fever pitch.

He writes:

> The Wanderers are, for the first time since their organization, possessors of the Stanley Cup, for, though they were beaten by the Ottawas at Dey's Arena Saturday night by 9 goals to 3, yet they won on the round, having defeated the Ottawas last Wednesday in Montreal by 9 goals to 1.
>
> A Titanic struggle was that of Saturday—one that stands out alone in the history of hockey in Canada. Enthusiasm never paralleled at a hockey match in Ottawa was witnessed—and later that enthusiasm was eclipsed.
>
> **A Ten Minutes' Cheer**
>
> The Ottawas achieved the impossible and then lost the advantage they had gained—and the Stanley Cup. They went into the game with the score 9 to 1 against, with eight goals to tie the Wanderers on the round, and with 9 goals to score to beat their rivals and retain the Cup.
>
> They did score 9 goals, but the Wanderers secured the first goal and, near the finish, the standing on the round was ten goals all. This nine goal feat by the Ottawas was supposed to be super-human, but it was accomplished. Then it was that the crowd of 5,000 went literally wild. Hats and overcoats were thrown recklessly in the air, vocal organs were strained to their utmost limit, embraces were given and returned boisterously by utter strangers— and His Most Noisy Majesty, Pandemonium, reigned for ten minutes.
>
> Not among the small Wanderer contingent though. It

sat back and gazed at the blue haze that hid the ceiling and thought of the day that the rent comes round. The boldest backer of the Wanderers would not have wagered a cancelled postage stamp on them at that stage.

The Cup Looked Safe

Ottawas 9, Wanderers 1, and the Ottawas playing their opponents off their feet. The Stanley Cup looking safe to remain in Canada's Capital and the Wanderers looked safe to lose the greatest advantage ever gained by a rival team over the redoubtable Ottawas. From the Wanderers standpoint all seemed lost, and to their supporters it was only a question of how many goals they would be beaten by.

And then the thunderbolt! That axiom—it is the unexpected that always happens— swung into the limelight and Ottawans were rendered speechless, were dazed by seeing their vaunted team that has made so many wonderful finishes, beaten out in the dying moments of the match.

Wanderers Woke Up

With ten minutes to play and the score 9 to 1 in their favor, the Ottawas apparently had a stranglehold, a half-Nelson and a bar-hold on the Stanley Cup. Then they faded away and the Wanderers, who might as well before this have been sitting up in the rafters smoking cigarettes, started in to advertise the fact that they could play hockey. With their reputation and the Governor General's silverware at stake, they took a brace, and, having plenty of reserve strength when the Ottawas were exhausted, they outplayed their opponents, and, before the crowd could realize it, they scored a goal that was up to their regular Wanderer standard and was absolutely brilliant.

That made it 9 to 2, gave the Wanderers a lead of one goal on the round, and loosened thirteen rivets in the Stanley Cup's base. Then it was that the Wanderers' rooters made it potent that they were alive. There were only about 500 of them, but a particularly aggressive tornado was as mild as a summer evening's zephyr compared with the disturbance they created. Let no one imagine for a minute that they behaved as though they were at a Sunday afternoon tea, because they didn't. There was no organized yell, simply a confusion of sounds that would have done credit to the most blatant boiler factory.

Ottawas Were Tired Out

The Wanderers did look good just about then. They were displaying, for the first time during the match, confidence in themselves, and were acting accordingly. Instead of letting the Ottawas do the bulk of the attacking, they turned the tables, and hometowners Pulford, Moore and goaltender Lesueur had enough trouble to wreck the happiest home. It was the Ottawas' turn to do the chasing and checking, and they hadn't the energy left in them to effectively perform the work demanded of them. Tired out by their sustained exertions, they had to bear the pain of seeing their antagonists snatch the laurels from their hands. It was all Wanderers at this period, and the majority of the rooters were stunned anew at the spectacle of the Montreal septet scoring again.

That made it 9 to 3, with the Wanderers going strong and the Stanley Cup in their grasp. Only a miracle could rob them of Lord Stanley's trophy, and the miracle didn't happen. Slowly for the Wanderers, but all too fast for the Ottawas, did the hands of the big rink clock move in their appointed circle, but move they did, and finally time was up, the game was over, and the championship of the Eastern Canada Amateur Hockey Association, the amateur hockey championship of the world, the generously advertised Stanley Cup, and bunches of contentment, belonged to Montreal.

Wonderful Cheering

For four years Wanderers had striven for that glorious moment. They had encountered hardships on and off the ice, and only Saturday night did they emerge victorious from their prolonged struggle, and if their ebullitions of delight were something to be remembered, that fact was not to be wondered at. It is no exaggeration to say that the Wanderers' rooters became absolutely frantic in their demonstrations of joy. The men yelled and the fairer Montrealers shrieked, and all the while the thousands of Ottawans looked on in sour silence. The Montreal contingent rushed on the ice and tried to catch the boys who wore the broad red band to congratulate them. The players, however, hurried off the ice and their admirers had to be content with shouting and flaunting their colors in the faces of the hockey fans of Ottawa.

Ottawa had had their innings when the score was 9 to 1 and they did not leave anything out that would be noticed. When the Wanderers turn came they just about established a record in the Capital for rooting. From the rink to the Russell [Hotel] the streets rang with the Wanderers' song, a defiant "O-T-T-A-W-A" occasionally breaking into the stream of rejoicings.

Ottawa could hardly believe that their famous team was at last beaten, and in the packed rotundas of the hotels explanations were swapped and condolences exchanged by the thousands. The one explanation that seemed to be the most popular was that the Ottawas had had too much hockey this winter and that they were not able to stand the strain of a hard hour's work as well as their opponents. This was true, though, for three quarters of the playing time the Ottawas had the Wanderers on the run, yet in the last quarter of an hour the Wanderers reversed the situation and scored, during the final moments of the contest, the goals that won the championship.

Ottawas Played Desperately

Had the Ottawas been able to maintain from start to finish the pace they set when the puck was first set in motion, it is extremely doubtful if the Wanderers would now hold the silverware. The Wanderers were dazzled by the swiftness of the Ottawas' attacks and could only lie back and defend their nets. The Ottawas bore in on the nets in a manner that might truthfully be termed desperate. They took daring chances when carrying the war into the enemy's territory, and were rewarded for their zeal by scoring goals when the Wanderers appeared to have frustrated the onslaughts. This scheme of attack held good until the Wanderers came into their own. Then the Ottawas got a taste of the medicine they had been ladling out with so free a hand.

The Wanderers would swoop down the ice three and four abreast and the determined efforts of Moore and Pulford to hold them were but futile. They could stop one or two men but not three or four, and the nets sagged twice and the Ottawas' glory was departed.

Details of the Game

From the drop of the puck the Ottawas went into the game

with rare zest and energy, and the Wanderers had to remain on the defensive, making a feeble rush now and again. On one of these rushes they had a shot at [goaltender] Lesueur, whom the puck struck on the back. It rolled down his side and before he could connect with it, it rolled into the nets and the standing on the round was 10 to 1 in the Wanderers' favor.

The Ottawas had nine goals to make up and they went at the job in a business-like way, and before half time they had three goals of the nine scored. The second half opened up in whirlwind fashion with a rush from the faceoff by Harry Smith, who wriggled through the entire Wanderer team and tallied on a neat side shot.

Soon the standing was even. Hats, scarves and galoshes flew down on the ice. There was a hullabaloo. "The Cup will stay in Ottawa" was the slogan. But the Wanderers took what the Ottawas had long been celebrated for—a brace—and in a few minutes Lester Patrick made two brilliant rushes and put two pucks past Lesueur and it was all over so far as the Ottawas were concerned. The Cup was slated for a new boarding house.

How Ottawa Feels

The departure of the Stanley Cup is regarded with mixed feelings at the Capital. The Ottawas held the Cup for three years and had to lead a strenuous life to do so, and for the past three weeks particularly their existence has been full of weariness. They had two Cup series—with Queens and Smiths Falls—sandwiched in between games in their regular league. Physically, they were about "all in," and though they were naturally sorry to lose the trophy, they felt grateful that the strain was over.

Such a well known lover of amateur sport as Mr. Denis Murphy, one of the patrons of the Ottawa Hockey Club, had the following to say about the Cup's journey to Montreal:

"In one way I am sorry our boys lost, but for their own sakes I think it is a good thing that the Cup is gone. They have undergone a most trying ordeal for the past three years and the strain has not done them any good. They have had to play so much hockey that there has been no sport for them. I have often told them that I wished someone would steal the Stanley Cup as it was hurting hockey and not helping it. The Ottawas have made a record that will probably never be equaled by any other hockey team but they have had a terrible time doing it, and the Wanderers will find that defending the Stanley Cup entails a most painful strain on them. If I had my way there would be no Stanley Cup and no hockey team would be compelled to play more than the scheduled games in the league to which it belongs."

Mr. Murphy's sentiments are those of many sportsmen in Ottawa and Montreal, but naturally the Wanderers are elated over becoming the holders of the silverware. The players are tickled so that their smiles can be seen a block away, and the executive not suffering from any sorrow brought on by the hockey situation.

The Players

The star of the game Saturday night was Billy Strachan, his cool, strong defense work being the attractive feature of the Wanderers' work. To show how effective Strachan was, it may be stated that while he was on the penitent bench for striking McGee, the Ottawas scored three goals. Strachan had the faculty for being on the spot where he was most needed. [Author's note: It might be argued that Strachan took a foolish penalty and his team was scored on three times while he was off the ice. Even so, the sportswriter named Strachan a bigger star than Harry Smith, who scored five goals for Ottawa.]

Flawless Frank McGee led all the Ottawa scorers over the season with 28 goals in a mere seven games played. In the playoffs for the Cup, McGee scored 17 goals in six games.

Lester Patrick was the best of the Wanderers' forwards, and was very much in the game from start to finish, and some of his dashes were exceedingly good to look on. Three he spoiled by shooting wide when he had fooled both Pulford and Moore. It was in the final stages when the game had to be won in short order that Patrick scintillated. He went down the ice, nursing the puck, sidestepping and dodging and had the Ottawa defense dazed.

Johnson was very aggressive in the last quarter of an hour, and was all over the ice with that sweeping stride that carried him along at marvellous speed. He took the puck the length of the rink many times and tired out the lagging Ottawas. He was hit in the face late in the game by Westwick and lost several teeth, and that seemed to put ginger into him.

The Ottawas rushes were not only pretty but eminently effective. Alf Smith, Frank McGee and Harry Smith worked like driven slaves to win the game, and every one of them, until, he became exhausted, worked in stellar fashion. They had everything that goes to make up a good hockey player, and the way they secured and maintained control of the puck was nothing short of wonderful.

Harry Smith was the best shot on the ice and the

accuracy and speed with which he drove the puck at Menard were worth remembering.

Lesueur made some clever saves. [Author's note: This was Percy Lesueur's first game for Ottawa, a fact that is not mentioned. Lesueur had been playing for Smiths Falls against Ottawa in the preceding week. Just a few days before this game, Ottawa dropped Billy Hague, their regular goaltender, victim of nine Wanderer goals in the first game, and replaced him with Lesueur.]

Before the Game

The demand for tickets exceeded the supply by thousands. The few hundred that were sent to Montreal were snapped up in jig time and could tickets have been obtained there would have been as many Montrealers at the game as there were Ottawas. As it was, 500 supporters accompanied the Wanderers to the Capital, and not half of them had tickets. They were met at the station by fully 1,000 Ottawans and among the latter were a few speculators who had a limited number of tickets to sell from $5 to $10, and these tickets were sold even at the extravagant prices mentioned.

Packed in Like Sardines

Dey's Arena has accommodation for 4,200 people at a pinch, but 5,000 must have been squeezed into it Saturday night. The standing room at the west end was literally jammed with a crowd that swayed like lush grass in a breeze. That the sides of the building were not forced out, or that someone's ribs were not caved in, was due to a kind Providence.

The seating accommodations and the promenade were taxed to the limit, as were the girders and eligible spaces that flies would hardly dare to cling to. Some youthful daredevils even climbed up on the roof and hung to the window ledges by their teeth. Before five o'clock the fans had begun to gather at the general admission door, and when the latter was opened there were enough people clamoring for entrance to fill the entire rink. Hundreds were turned away, and many of these had traveled miles to see the game.

Special trains were run from Montreal and Cornwall, and these were crowded, as were the regular trains coming from every direction. Some came from Toronto to see the game, only to fail to get into the rink. About all the fun they had was after the match, when the celebrations were in full swing.

The Governor General Arrives

It was just a few minutes before game time when Earl Grey and Lady Grey arrived at the rink, and as they walked across the ice to their private box, Wanderer and Ottawa rooters united in cheering them to the echo. The Governor General acknowledged this tribute to his popularity by raising his hat and bowing and Lady Grey by bowing and smiling. In passing, it may be stated that the Governor General is a hockey enthusiast of the first water.

When Harry Smith ripped through the Wanderers and scored his 5th goal the Governor General called him over to his box and shook his hand, and congratulated him on his wonderful play. Earlier in the game, in a scuffle for the puck along the boards, Ernie Johnson's stick accidentally crashed through the hat of the Governor General.

The teams apparently were waiting for Earl Grey to reach the rink. The players skated around for ten minutes or so until the goal judges were recruited from the crowd.

41

It was the soft ice of the second half that had much to do with the Ottawas' defeat, as it sapped their strength and left them helpless when the final test came. Though the ice was cleared at half time, and though the temperature outside was below zero, yet the warm breath of the big crowd had the effect of making it so slushy that the players found it extremely difficult to keep the puck under control. They skated over it and lost it frequently when rushing. This was especially true of the Ottawas, Alf Smith being the only forward who had any luck when trying to worm his way through the opposing line.

Ottawa won the game 9–3, but Wanderers took the round 12–10.

When the same teams met in Ottawa the following season, the writer described the Stanley Cup fever that gripped the city:

A crowd of men and boys, estimated at over one thousand, waited in line for hours in zero temperatures hoping to buy tickets for the championship match. Many in the crowd waited all night. In the jam this morning, windows were broken, hats and coats torn and destroyed, and the police had to use their batons freely to quell the disorder. The plate glass windows in the offices of the Bang Coal Company were smashed in the struggles of the crowd. The police had to fight their way through the mob to prevent further damage. This followed news that tickets to the game would not be sold until mid-afternoon at Dey's rink. Only a few tickets were to be had and windows of the arena were broken by chunks of ice thrown by the disappointed fans.

The Arrogant Wanderers

When a team compiles a winning record that earns plaudits like "incredible" and "phenomenal," it sometimes becomes difficult for the players to keep their heads in their hats. A team that wins 27 games and loses only three can find itself having to deal with arrogance and swollen egos. Such was the case with the mighty Montreal Wanderers a century ago.

In 1908, after three superb seasons in a row during which they'd won 27 times in 30 regular-season outings, the mighty Wanderers began to think they were the Lords of Hockey—an unbeatable combination. They had sailed through the 10-game 1907 schedule undefeated, scoring 105 goals — an average of more than 10 per game, a record that has never been matched by any of hockey's hottest teams. Although—get this—in that same season, the Montreal Vics came close. They scored 101 goals in ten games.

Ernie Russell, the Wanderers' top scorer, scored 42 goals in the nine games he played—over four goals per game! In three seasons, playing in 24 games, Russell tallied 84 goals. Try to match that scoring burst, Sidney!

The mighty Wanderers lost a midseason Stanley Cup challenge to Kenora that winter, but won it back two months later.

In the Stanley Cup matches the following season, the Wanderers easily defeated challengers from Ottawa and Winnipeg. Then came a third challenge late in the year—a surprise bid from a Toronto team.

"Why, Toronto is no match for us," said the Wanderers. "They have one player who can score—Newsy Lalonde. After Newsy, look at their lineup. There's not another Toronto player who can compete at our level."

But the Stanley Cup trustees insisted that Toronto had the right to challenge the champions. It would be a two-game series for the Stanley Cup.

"The games will be a travesty," the Wanderers argued. "No one will pay to see such a series because we are too strong. We'll more than double the score against Toronto."

Double the score?

The Wanderers pestered the Cup trustees to schedule only a single game against Toronto. "After we pound them over 60 minutes, nobody will come to a second game," they predicted. "And we want home ice for the game. We're the champions, are we not?"

The trustees bowed to the Wanderers' demands.

On March 14, 1908, fans thirsty for playoff action filled the arena for the game. Many were willing to bet huge sums of money on the Wanderers' boast that they would "double the score" against the challengers.

But the Toronto boys proved to be much worthier opponents than the Wanderers had anticipated. The game seesawed back and forth, and the score was tied four times. Wanderer fans grew angry, because the hometown team had promised plenty of goals and now they were being held in check. A lot of money would be lost if they didn't pull up their socks.

During a break in the play, a group of anxious fans called the Wanderers over to the boards, including goalie Riley Hern. "You boys better double the score like you promised," said one of the bettors. "We've got a lot of cash riding on the outcome."

Another fan waved a roll of bills. "We'll throw a big bonus your way," he promised, "but you've got to double the score."

While this conversation was in progress, the referee grew irritated. "Enough talk. Let's play," he barked. He dropped the puck at centre ice before the Wanders could scramble into position. Toronto ace Newsy Lalonde snapped it up and fired a long shot into the Wanderers' empty net.

"But we weren't ready," screamed the Wanderers. "We were talking."

"Too bad," replied the referee. "Goal counts."

The empty-net goal angered the Wanderers, and the promise of bonus money inspired them. They whacked in a pair of goals and won the game 6–4. But their splurge wasn't enough. They had failed on their promise to "double the score" and their fans were furious.

"We lost a lot of money on those egotistical know-it-alls," said one.

The Wanderers got their come-uppance in 1909.

As four-time winners of the Stanley Cup, they were shocked when the Cup trustees ordered them to turn the trophy over to the Ottawa Hockey Club, champions of the Eastern Canada Hockey Association. Ottawa, paced by Marty Walsh, had beaten the Wanderers in two of three games played between the bitter rivals that season, during which Walsh enjoying his finest campaign, scoring 42 goals in 12 games.

"Ottawa doesn't deserve the Cup," protested manager Dickie Boon of the Wanderers. "We're still the better team."

"Just do as we say," countered the trustees.

In time, the Cup was shipped to Ottawa in a box. The Ottawa players eagerly pulled the trophy from its container and held it aloft.

"Those Montreal bastards have ruined it," exclaimed one Ottawa player. "Look! They've scratched their names all over the inside of the bowl. They were supposed to put their team name and the year they held the Cup on a small silver plate on the base of the trophy. They totally ignored the plate and defaced a great trophy. They should be tarred and feathered. What they did is outrageous."

There was no doubt the Stanley Cup had been abused. Someone in the Wanderers' camp, using a metal instrument, had scrawled their names in large letters inside the bowl of the trophy. Some of the signatures didn't even belong—they were from players who had been Wanderers two and three years earlier.

Hockey fans everywhere condemned the Wanderers for defiling Lord

Stanley's gift to hockey. But the Montrealers shrugged off the criticism and refused to apologize. Meanwhile, Ottawa officials hired a silversmith to erase the signatures and restore the famous trophy to its original condition.

Flu Epidemic Brings 1919 Series to a Close

On April 2, 1919, hockey officials in Seattle reluctantly cancelled what remained of the Stanley Cup final series between the hometown Metropolitans and the visiting Montreal Canadiens. The reason? The players were so ill they were staggering around the ice, out on their feet. The dreaded flu pandemic that raged across North America that year, was taking an alarming toll on the players involved.

It was estimated that the disease killed more people around the world than the First World War. The virus killed at least 50 million people world-wide, and possibly as many as 100 million. The flu, which caused an estimated 600,000 deaths in the U.S. and Canada, was particularly lethal for relatively healthy young adults. One survivor, William Sardo, Jr.—in his mid-90s—remembers pine caskets being stacked in the living room of his family home. "Some folks took ill in the morning and were dead by nightfall," says Sardo. "People who were known to be infected were threatened with a $50 fine—big money in that era—if they were seen in public. Some people blamed the Germans for starting the disease."

Five players on the Canadiens' roster were reported to be seriously ill with the disease, and officials, realizing it was a life-and-death situation, threw in the towel. The series was called off after five games, each team having won twice and one game (the fourth) having ended in a tie. One more game would have decided the title.

The fourth game required an hour and 40 minutes of overtime and ended in a scoreless tie. It was described as the greatest game ever played in the west. The fifth game also went to almost a full period of overtime before Montreal won by a 4–3 score.

During the overtime, Cully Wilson of Seattle fell to the ice in exhaustion while Joe Hall of Montreal also collapsed and could not continue. Hall was rushed to a nearby hospital that was jammed with flu victims. Following the game, manager George Kennedy, Canadiens captain Newsy Lalonde, and teammates Billy Couture, Louis Berlinquette, and Jack McDonald were all confined to their rooms in the Georgian Hotel.

Hospital space was at a premium and they could not be moved there. Temperatures of the men ranged from 101 to 105 degrees. Only Didier Pitre, Odie Cleghorn, and Georges Vezina of the Canadiens were not afflicted. It's amazing that half the roster was not wiped out. Medical men theorized that the Canadiens contracted the disease in Victoria, where the players had mingled with members of the Victoria hockey club, many of whom were recovering from the devastating illness.

A Seattle reporter wrote: "Never in the history of the Stanley Cup series has the championship been so beset with hard luck as this one. Of the nineteen players engaged in it, hardly one of them has gone through it without some bad luck, injury or illness.

"Lengthy overtime periods taxed the vitality of the players to such an extent that they were in poor condition to fight off the disease.

"Today, workmen began tearing up the arena ice floor to convert the building into a roller skating rink. The fact that the ice was being taken up settled all arguments as to whether or not the series would be continued."

A few days later, on April 5, "Bad" Joe Hall of the Canadiens, too ill to accompany his teammates back to Montreal, succumbed to the disease in a Seattle hospital. Hockey's toughest, most penalized player had battled the disease for four days. He was 36 years old and had been coaxed into playing one final season. Later, back in Montreal, manager George Kennedy, who was sometimes known as George Kendall, also had his life snuffed out by the disease.

Joe Hall was one of the most famous of hockey's pioneer players and one of the few to be charged by police for his actions on the ice. In his final season, playing against Toronto, he was involved in a vicious stick-swinging incident with Alf Skinner, another star of the era. Both men were arrested by Toronto police and charged with disorderly conduct. In court, the charges were dismissed.

The Canadiens appeared to run into bad luck whenever they met Seattle. Two years earlier, in the spring of 1917, when the Canadiens played the Seattle Metropolitans for the Stanley Cup, they ran into a buzz saw named Bernie Morris who was called "the man most responsible for bringing the Stanley Cup across the border." During the regular season in the Pacific Coast Hockey Association, Morris had scored 37 goals in 24 games, including a five-goal game against Vancouver.

In the Stanley Cup battles against Montreal, Morris produced a three-goal game in the opening match, but his team lost by a score of 8–4. In game two he scored twice in a 6–1 pounding of the Habs. In this game Newsy Lalonde, the great Montreal star, butt-ended the referee and escaped with a match penalty and a small fine. Morris collected his second hat trick of the series in game three, a 4–1 win for Seattle. He was sensational in game four, scoring a record six goals in a 9–1 rout. If there had been a Conn Smythe Trophy in that era, Morris would have won it handily with his 14 goals in four games. More than any other player, he helped the Seattle Metropolitans take possession of the Stanley Cup, making them the first U.S.-based champion. The five-foot, seven-inch 145-pounder was charged with draft evasion by the U.S. Army and missed part of the 1918–19 season and all of the 1919–20 campaign. All charges were later dropped. Morris scored one goal in the NHL—with the Boston Bruins late in his career.

Clancy's Feat Will Never Be Matched

Hockey Hall of Famer Frank "King" Clancy was one of my favourite story-tellers. As a kid in Ottawa—this was before the NHL was born in 1917—he used to sneak into Dey's Arena to watch the famous Senators play Stanley Cup games. He'd sneak through a hole in the wall into the men's room. "But I had to be careful," he chuckled. "The guys inside the rink would piss into a trough, and the piss would flow down the trough and through a hole leading outside. If I sneaked through the wrong hole I was in trouble. And sometimes the piss would freeze and make better ice outside the rink than inside. But we never skated on it. Nobody did. It would be an awful yellow colour."

Years later, Clancy was still a teenager when he joined the famed Senators as a 135-pound defenceman. That was in the 1921–22 season. In 1923, his sophomore year, he took part in one of the roughest playoff series ever played—a brutal two-game matchup with the Canadiens.

"Talk about rough!" he recalled. "It was murder on ice. I had broken in the year before—a skinny little defenceman—and I'm involved in a two-game playoff with the Montreal Canadiens. Their manager, Leo Dandurand, along with a couple of his pals, had purchased the Montreal franchise some time earlier for $11,000. What a bargain that was!"

One of our players, Frank Nighbor from Pembroke, set a mark that season that has never been equalled and never will be. He played in six straight games without leaving the ice. And he scored a goal in each of those games.

But let me tell you about rough.

We won the first game with Montreal 2–0, but it was wild and scary. Cleghorn and Couture on the Montreal defence tried to kill us. When Cy Denneny scored a goal, Billy Couture sneaked up from behind him and cracked him over the head with his stick. They carried Cy off to get a dozen stitches and he had a concussion. Cleghorn then knocked Hitchman unconscious with a cross check. Oh, it was vicious. Those two were killers. When the referee tossed Cleghorn, the crowd went wild. They threw everything on the ice—nuts, bolts, and bottles. Hats and programs. Shoes and boots. Some of them tried to attack the referee—a fellow named Lou Marsh. We were lucky to get out of Montreal alive.

Leo Dandurand did something that truly amazed us after that game. He was so disgusted with the actions of Cleghorn and Couture that he suspended them for the next game. He wanted to win that series, wanted it badly, but not if it meant someone was going to be murdered on the ice. And the Habs did beat us back on our ice, but we won the series because we scored more goals. I can still see Cy Denneny, wearing a big bandage on his head, scoring our only goal, even though he was still dizzy from the concussion and should have been home in bed. Or in the hospital.

We all took a big sigh of relief and headed off by train to Vancouver, where there were two challengers waiting to meet us.

We arrived in Vancouver stiff and tired after the long train ride, and a few hours later we were on the ice facing the Vancouver Maroons. Close to 10,000 fans turned out to see the first game in the series, which we won 1–0 when Punch Broadbent scored a goal with time running out. We lost the second game 4–1 and suffered another rash of injuries, which slowed us down. In the third game, which we won 3–2, Broadbent scored a pair of goals while Frank Nighbor scored the winner.

Up to this point I was a substitute in the series. But after we suffered all those injuries, I found myself playing everywhere. Coach Petey Green threw me out on the right wing, then I played centre and left wing, and of course I played defence. Why, I got more ice time than any of my teammates.

Despite our crippled lineup, we eliminated Vancouver in five games. The Vancouver fans gave us quite an ovation when the series ended and Frank Patrick called us the greatest hockey team he had ever seen.

But we were only halfway to the Stanley Cup. Waiting around to meet us was a team from Edmonton, and three days later we squared off with them in the same rink. The Edmonton club, with stars like Duke Keats and Bullet Joe Simpson, had been willing to travel west for a chance at the Stanley Cup. Too bad they got us.

Keats was the big cheese. He'd scored eight goals in one game against Saskatoon and there was talk that he'd skate our Frank Nighbor right out of the rink. As it turned out, we won the opener on Cy Denneny's overtime goal and Nighbor proved himself to be every inch the equal of Keats.

It was in this game that I had the biggest surprise of my life. At one point, our goaltender, Clint Benedict, pulled the feet out from under an Edmonton player and drew a penalty. In those days, the goalie had to serve his time in the box. Well, Clint threw his goalie stick to me and barked, "Here, kid. Take care of this goal until I get back!"

Now, playing in goal was not my cup of tea. I'd never had any desire to be a goalie. But there I was, stuck in the net and hanging onto Benedict's big stick.

But somebody had to do it and he'd singled out me. So after playing all the other positions in that game, I tended goal for a couple of minutes. At one point an Edmonton player shot the puck close to my net and I scrambled out of my net and fell on it.

Mickey Ion, the referee, skated up to me and warned me, "The next time you do that, kid, you're going off!" I didn't argue with him because at that time I didn't open my mouth to any of the referees.

Years later, the story of my goaltending in the Stanley Cup finals was given a twist here and there. I've seen it in print where I made several fine saves. Another writer said I grabbed the puck and dashed up the ice with it on my goal stick and fired a shot at the opposing goalie. The truth of it is I didn't make a single stop.

It's not in any record book, but no other player has ever played every position on the ice in a Stanley Cup game. And it'll never happen again.

We won that series with Edmonton two games to none, with Punch Broadbent scoring the only goal in the second game.

Capturing the hockey championship of the world was the greatest thing that ever happened to me. After earning $800 for the season and then collecting $750 in one shot for the three playoff series—I was a very rich man!

Here's another Stanley Cup memory. This goes back to when I was a Maple Leaf. The Leafs met the Boston Bruins in the playoffs in the spring of 1936.

Again, it was one of those two-game, total-goals-to-count series. Well, the Bruins jumped in front by shutting us out 3–0 in Boston. Left us peeking out from behind the old eight ball.

In game two, back in Toronto, the Bruins opened fast and took a 1–0 lead. It sure looked like curtains for the Leafs. Eddie Shore was the big cheese for the Bruins, the best player on the ice in both games. So I decided to try and get under his skin and maybe throw him off his game. In the Leaf dressing room before the third period, I told my teammates, "Don't worry, men. I've got Shore in my hip pocket."

After the period started, Shore was caught for some infraction, and that made him furious. He was headed for the penalty box when I skated up to him and said, "Geez, Eddie. That was a rotten call. You didn't do a thing to deserve that penalty. The referee must be out to get you, to show you up." My words must have registered with Shore because suddenly he wheeled around, laid his stick on the puck, and fired it at referee Odie Cleghorn. Hit him right in the backside. Bull's-eye! Now, Cleghorn was as tough as old shoe leather and he wouldn't stand for any nonsense from Shore. He hollered, "Okay, wise guy. That'll cost you another 10 minutes in the box."

What a break for us! With Shore in the penalty box, the Bruins sagged. By the time he got back, we'd scored four goals to tie the round. I got one of the goals, I remember. Then we scored two more goals and went on to wallop the Bruins 8–3 in that game. Over two games, we outscored them 8–6 and knocked them right out of the playoffs.

Shore was such a character. Did you know he used to skate out on the ice before games in Boston wearing a long gold dressing gown over his uniform? What a showman! And the music would blare "Hail to the Chief" while he waltzed around the ice.

Of course I loved to needle him. I'd skate up to him and say, "You look so lovely in that gown, Eddie. I hope you'll be wearing it in the game. I'd love to see you get all tangled up in it and fall into the boards and then start crying for a penalty."

He'd just glare at me and say, "I'm going to kill you tonight, Clancy."

And I'd say, "You try it, Eddie, if you're not afraid of taking a good licking in front of all your adoring fans."

Of course, we both knew I couldn't lick a Popsicle. I think I was in a hundred fights and never won a single one of them.

But I must say this. Shore was a fabulous player and later on he became a good friend of mine. I guess by then he'd forgotten all the nasty things I said to him on the ice.

First Series on the West Coast

Thanks to the Patrick brothers, Lester and Frank, a pair of hockey visionaries, big-league hockey soon became a major attraction on the Pacific Coast. The Patricks, dynamic young men in their twenties, had returned to British Columbia after playing the 1910 season with the Renfrew Millionaires of the National Hockey Association. With their father's promise of financial backing, they decided to form a new league that would attract the best players in the world—and would involve cities that definitely wanted a chance to win the Stanley Cup.

The usual number of skeptics came romping out of the woods.

"You fellows are crazy," the Patricks were told. "The winters out here are often balmy. Natural ice is unpredictable. You'll be playing your games on water—wearing rubber boots, not skates."

"Then we'll build arenas with artificial ice," the boys responded. "Just watch us."

And that's what they did. Two arenas sprang up in Vancouver and Victoria—the first artificial ice rinks in Canada. Many of the 24 players (eight to a team) recruited by the Patricks helped lay the 15 miles of pipe needed to freeze water into ice. "We were young and anxious to play," Walter Smaill recalled years later. "We worked long hours to get those arenas open. I nearly lost my life working on the roof. A gust of wind blew me to the edge and I hung there suspended for a few anxious minutes. Finally, a workman threw me a rope and yanked me to safety."

The building in Vancouver, with seats for 10,000, was second in size only to Madison Square Garden in New York. The arena in Victoria seated about 6,000. The Pacific Coast Hockey Association was born with franchises in Victoria (the Aristocrats), Vancouver (the Maroons and later Millionaires), and New Westminster (the Royals). The first PCHA game was played on January 5, 1912. The Patricks were owners, managers, coaches, players, rule-makers—and referees if need be. In fact, players in the league, many of them top stars recruited from eastern teams, agreed to act as referees on nights they weren't performing. The extra money helped, even though the Patricks generously paid them as much or more than they could get elsewhere. Only two dozen players filled the three rosters, sixteen of them imports. New Westminster won the league title in 1911–12, and Newsy Lalonde was the leading scorer with 27 goals in 15 games.

"We filled those new buildings every night we played," Smaill recalled. "And it was exciting hockey. I was paid a thousand dollars for the season, and, like everyone else, I played the full 60 minutes."

The coast league did not challenge for the Cup that season, but the following year, Quebec, the Stanley Cup champs, journeyed west and played three exhibition games against Victoria. Victoria defeated the visitors easily in two of the three games played.

The following year, Victoria travelled east to play Toronto, but they were not officially Cup challengers. It seems they had neglected to submit a formal challenge. It turned out not to matter. They lost by scores of 6–0 and 5–2.

In 1914–15, three teams competed in the PCHA: Vancouver, Victoria, and Portland. The Oregon city had gained possession of the former New Westminster team, which now went by the name the Portland Rosebuds. Some fans scoffed at the name at first, but they soon got used to it—not unlike modern-day fans who became accustomed to watching the Mighty Ducks. The move raised the possibility that a U.S.–based team might compete for the Stanley Cup, though Lord Stanley had donated the trophy for the championship of Canada.

Vancouver was by far the most powerful club, finishing with a 13–4 record and scoring 115 goals while allowing just 71. Vancouver's Mickey MacKay led all scorers with 34 goals in 17 games.

The trustees for the Stanley Cup announced in early March that a challenge from Vancouver had been accepted and ordered Ottawa, the eastern champs, to journey west to defend the trophy. It was the first Stanley Cup series played west of Winnipeg.

Vancouver sought permission to make a roster change for the series. They wanted Victoria's Lester Patrick (a league founder and an all-star player) to replace the injured Si Griffis. Ottawa protested so strongly that Frank Patrick, Vancouver's manager and the league president, withdrew the request. "I think we can beat Ottawa without you, Lester," he told his brother. As it turned out, he was right. The Vancouver club needed no further strengthening.

The games were played on the slick artificial ice at the Denman Arena in Vancouver. On March 22, more than 7,000 fans turned out to see the first game in the best-of-three series played under western rules (seven-man hockey as opposed to six). Mickey MacKay and Fred Taylor skated rings around the Ottawa champions, and the Millionaires captured the first game handily by a score of 6–2.

In the second game, played under eastern (six-man) rules, Taylor collected a hat trick and Frank "The Pembroke Peach" Nighbor scored twice. Again, it was no contest as the Millionaires walloped the visitors 8–3.

The third and final game was another rout, Vancouver winning 12–3, one of the highest scores in Cup history. Ottawa held Taylor in check, but his teammates were unstoppable. Barney Stanley scored four goals while MacKay and Nighbor each scored three.

The Millionaires were happy to receive a share of the playoff profits— $300 per man. The losers were handed $200 each.

And the Patricks were delighted. In a short time, they had fashioned a new league and brought the Stanley Cup west. They had introduced new rules and innovations and rejected others.

The Patricks had been among the first to ridicule rules changes suggested earlier by T. Emmett Quinn of the Ottawa club. Quinn had proposed reducing the puck to half its size and painting it green. He suggested that players should carry money in their hip pockets in order to pay fines on the spot. And he wanted referees to take players aside when they were caught slashing, holding, or interfering with opponents, then have a good chat with the offender and try to reform him.

II. The NHL Takes Control

Hamilton's Cup Hopes Shattered by Player Revolt

My father, Leslie McFarlane, the first author of the Hardy Boys books under the pen name Franklin W. Dixon, was a sportswriter in the 1920s, covering hockey for the *Sudbury Star*. In the '20s and '30s, Sudbury produced many star players. Among them were Red Green and his brother Shorty. They would play in the NHL for the Hamilton Tigers and the New York Americans.

In the spring of 1925, the brothers came agonizingly close to a Stanley Cup victory. But an argument over a few measly dollars killed their chances. In one of my dad's diaries written in the '30s, he mentions Shorty Green and how he came by our house in Haileybury one day: "Shorty showed up in his new car and took Brian for a ride. The youngster was thrilled."

I'm sure I was. But I was too young to remember it.

Imagine a big-league hockey star driving you around in his new car and being too young to remember it!

Red and Shorty Green figured prominently in a huge debacle that preceded the 1925 Stanley Cup playoffs.

In 1924–25, the NHL added two new franchises: the Boston Bruins and Montreal Maroons. They joined the Hamilton Tigers, Toronto St. Pats, Montreal Canadiens, and Ottawa Senators. The 24-game schedule was beefed up to 30 games, and the six extra games brought pay hikes to players on three of the four existing clubs. The cheapskate Hamilton Tigers, owned by the Abso-Pure Ice Company and Percy Thompson, refused to compensate their players for the extra workload, even though the Tigers finished atop the NHL standings and earned a bye into the NHL finals.

After a season-ending loss to Montreal on March 9, the Tigers held a team meeting on the train headed back to Hamilton. They decided not to suit up for another game until each man was paid a total of $200 for the six extra games they'd played.

Billy Burch, who was born Harry Burch and was voted the NHL's most valuable player, met with Percy Thompson and told him the players would not compromise and would not back down.

"We'll see about that," Thompson replied angrily. "I won't give you fellows an extra penny."

The players remained obstinate. "Then we're officially on strike," Red Green told reporters. "To hell with the playoffs and the Stanley Cup."

The player revolt—the first strike of a professional sports team—became front-page news. NHL president Frank Calder sided with Thompson. He immediately suspended the Tigers, fined each man $200, and stated that the winner of the Montreal–Toronto series would compete against the western champions in the Stanley Cup finals (Montreal would lose to Victoria).

The player revolt cost the Tigers a chance for the Cup. And they never got another one. Before the next season rolled around, New York investors— one of them nefarious bootlegger "Big Bill" Dwyer—purchased the Hamilton franchise for $75,000. The franchise was shifted to Madison Square Garden, where it surfaced under a new name: the New York Americans.

The Hamilton players, so the story goes, before being reinstated, were ordered to apologize personally to President Calder for their mercenary attitude. "And don't forget to pay your fines," he warned them.

Most fans are surprised to discover that Hamilton—for a brief time— had the best team in the NHL. If they need proof, there is a large team photo of the long-forgotten Tigers in the concourse at Copps Coliseum.

As for the rebellious Shorty Green, his descendants may want to kick me for questioning his induction into the Hockey Hall of Fame in 1962. Family friend or not, his inclusion is surprising. Green played in a mere 103 NHL games over four seasons and scored a modest 33 goals and 53 points. Those don't sound like Hall of Fame numbers to me. But I refuse to be a detractor of a man who treated me to a drive in his new car. No way.

Perhaps "Big Bill" Dwyer deserves a postscript as well.

In the '20s, Dwyer dominated bootlegging in New York. Partnered with notorious criminals like Owney Madden and Frank Costello, he ran an illegal bootlegging operation that stretched from Europe to New York. He bribed politicians, police, and Coast Guard officials to assure there'd be no interference.

He not only owned the Americans but he later secretly owned the Pittsburgh Pirates, although the NHL would list boxer Benny Leonard as the owner.

Dwyer often tried to rig NHL games by hiring dishonest pals as goal judges. They were instructed to flash the red light if the puck came anywhere close to the opposing team's goal line.

He was the first NHL owner—but not the last—to serve jail time: a two-year sentence for attempting to bribe members of the Coast Guard.

The Silver-Haired Saviour

Surely you've heard the story of Lester Patrick and how he became the most famous—and one of the oldest—substitute goalies in Stanley Cup history. If you haven't, you've missed one of my favourite playoff tales.

In the summer of 1926, when the New York Rangers were preparing to make their NHL debut, Lester Patrick was hired to mould the team into a hockey powerhouse. Patrick, nicknamed the Silver Fox for his mane of white hair, had been a famous player, coach, and hockey innovator for many years. He and his brother Frank had organized the first professional league in Western Canada: the Pacific Coast Hockey Association. They had arranged for the first artificial ice plants to be installed in their arenas and had signed many of the best players in the world to play in their league. In 1925, a few months before joining the Rangers, Lester had led the Victoria Cougars to a stunning Stanley Cup victory over the Montreal Canadiens.

In 1926–27, Lester had immediate success with the Rangers, guiding them to first place in their division in their very first season. But it took another year before he was able to bring New York its first Stanley Cup. And he played a much bigger role in that historic victory than he ever could have imagined.

In the best-of-five finals in 1928, the Rangers clashed with the Montreal Maroons. The Rangers had been banished from Madison Square Garden because the annual circus had come to town, so all of the games were scheduled to be played in Montreal.

The Maroons opened with a 2–0 shutout over the Rangers. In game two, late in the second period, Ranger goalie Lorne Chabot was struck over the eye by a Nels Stewart shot. There were no goalie masks in those days, and Chabot was carried off on a stretcher.

Another missing link was the absence of backup goaltenders (teams didn't carry them), and so Lester Patrick was in a jam. Who would take over for Chabot?

Referee Mike Rodden told Patrick, "I'll give you 10 minutes to find a another goalie—and not a minute more."

In the Ranger dressing room, two of the team's stars, Frank Boucher and Bill Cook, said, half-kidding, "Lester, looks like you'll have to don the pads yourself."

Patrick was 44 years old, well past his prime. But he had little choice. He said, "I'll do it, boys, but you've got to promise to backcheck like hell."

The Rangers vowed to check the Maroons dizzy while Patrick struggled into Chabot's heavy goaltending gear. When he waddled out onto the ice, the Montreal fans roared with laughter. The white-haired coach didn't look very graceful on his skates. But when play began, he stopped every shot thrown his way. Well, almost every shot.

After the Rangers' Bill Cook scored in the third period to give New York a 1–0 lead, the Maroons' Nels Stewart rifled a shot past Patrick to tie the score.

"Sorry, boys," said Patrick. "I should have had it."

The old man made no more mistakes and the game went into overtime. At the seven-minute mark, Frank Boucher whipped in the winning goal. Rangers 2, Maroons 1. The Rangers mobbed their coach-turned-goalie and congratulated him on "a fantastic performance."

Patrick said "No, no, no" when asked if he'd be playing in the rest of the series. "I could never do that again. I barely survived out there."

Patrick brought up a minor leaguer, rookie Joe Miller, who allowed only three goals in the remaining three games and was as big a goaltending hero as

Patrick when the Rangers skated off with their first Stanley Cup.

Miller, the novice netminder, would never get close to the Stanley Cup again. Nor would he ever show similar brilliance in regular-season play. He performed with four NHL clubs over four seasons and left the pro scene with a dismal record of 24 wins and 87 losses.

Patrick left with a perfect 1–0 record and a goals-against average of 1.30.

Let me add a postscript. The most disappointed playoff performer that spring was goaltender Clint Benedict of the Maroons. In game after game, he was sensational. And he came away a loser. In the first round, a two-game series against Ottawa, Benedict shut out the Senators 1–0 in game one and was almost as stingy in game two, winning 2–1. Then he faced the first-place Montreal Canadiens in another two-game series. His Maroons tied the first game 2–2 and won the second 1–0. In the final series against the Rangers, Benedict racked up his third playoff shutout in the opener, winning 1–0. Game two, a 2–1 Ranger triumph, was the game in which coach Patrick took over in goal and skated off with a 2–1 victory. Benedict bounced back with his fourth playoff shutout (2–0) in game three, but the Rangers, with Miller in goal, returned the compliment and shut down the Maroons 1–0 in game four. New York captured game five 2–1 and won the Stanley Cup.

Benedict compiled four shutouts in nine games and allowed a mere eight goals. His near-perfect netminding was reflected in his goals against average- a miniscule 0.89. It was a brilliant playoff run. Unfortunately, not brilliant enough to get his name on the Stanley Cup.

Nobody blamed Benedict for the Maroons' defeat. But nobody showered him with praise, either. Everyone was captivated by Lester Patrick's pinch-hitting performance.

Bruins Win Their First Cup

When the 1928–29 NHL season opened, the Boston Bruins introduced a new goaltender with the unlikely name of Cecil.

Cecil "Tiny" Thompson, a kid from the town of Sandon, British Columbia, was purchased "sight unseen" by manager Art Ross to replace aging Hal Winkler. Veterans Eddie Shore and Lionel Hitchman were at their peak on defence. Aubrey "Dit" Clapper and Dutch Gainor, along with Ralph "Cooney" Weiland, formed the Dynamite Line—a high-scoring trio. Ross felt he had to gamble with a youngster in goal.

During the season, the Bruins introduced two U.S. college stars: George Owen, a Harvard grad, and former Dartmouth star Myles Lane, acquired from the Rangers. It was the season in which Eddie Shore missed the Bruins' train to Montreal by a few minutes, borrowed a friend's car, and drove all night through a blizzard, arriving at the Forum just in time to score the only goal of the match.

The Bruins tied a league record for most wins in a season (26) and scored the most goals (89). They finished two points behind the Canadiens in the overall standings and faced the Habs and their ace goaltender, George Hainsworth (22 shutouts in 44 games—still a big league record), in the opening round of the playoffs—a best-of-three affair.

Rookie Tiny Thompson came through with stellar back-to-back 1–0 shutouts in the first two games played in Boston. These stunning victories were followed by a 3–2 Boston win at the Montreal Forum and the Habs were toast.

When the Bruins arrived back in Boston, they were accorded the greatest reception for a Boston team—any Boston team—in history. And the Stanley Cup was still a series away!

For the first time in NHL history, two American teams, the Bruins and the Rangers, met in the best-of-three final series for the Stanley Cup. Boston captured the first game on home ice, 2–0, behind Thompson's superb goaltending. Two nights later, at Madison Square Garden, Dr. Bill Carson scored with less than two minutes to play in regulation time to give the Bruins a 2–1 victory and the Stanley Cup. Rookie Thompson had played in all five postseason games, recorded three shutouts, and given up a mere three goals. His goals-against average for the playoffs was 0.60.

Another wild celebration greeted the Bruins on their return to Boston, and a few days later, at a gala affair at the Copley Plaza Hotel, the players gathered for a victory party. Team president Charles Adams divvied up $35,000 in bonus money while the players surprised Adams with an unusual present: a two-foot bronze bear imported from Russia. Manager Art Ross received a set of golf clubs.

Ross expressed his appreciation for the loyalty his players had displayed all season. "There has never been a professional team," he said, "where there has been less bickering, fewer jealousies, and better spirit. You men deserve to be the Stanley Cup champions."

In 1947, Art Ross donated a trophy to hockey, to be awarded each year to the player who leads the league in scoring. The first winner of the Art Ross Trophy was Montreal's Elmer Lach, who enjoyed a 61-point season. Wayne Gretzky has won the trophy a record 10 times. His personal best was in 1985–86, when he amassed an astonishing 215 points. Gretzky is the only scoring champ to top 200 points in a season, and he did it four times.

Trivia buffs may know that Tiny Thompson, during the 1935-36 season, became the first NHL goaltender to register an assist in a game. His shutout total is extraordinary—81 of them in a 12-year career spanning 553 games. Terry Sawchuk's long-standing record of 103 shutouts was compiled over 21 seasons and 971 games.

The Longest Playoff Games

Bleary-eyed, the fan puts a nickel in the slot and calls his wife. He wakes her up.

"Dear, I can't come home just yet. It's not over yet."

"What's not over? Where are you? It's the middle of the night. It's after two. You've been drinking again, haven't you?"

"No, dear. I'm at the hockey game. At the Forum."

"Don't you lie to me. You left the house at seven. Hockey games don't last seven hours. You get right home!"

"No, dear. I'm not coming home. This is the longest hockey game ever played. I'm watching history tonight. The damn game may go on until dawn. And I'm not coming home until it's over."

He slams down the receiver.

That could have been the gist of a conversation between a man and his wife on that night in 1936, when the longest game in Stanley Cup history was played to a finish at the Montreal Forum. The game began on May 24 and finished on May 25. The Detroit Red Wings and Montreal Maroons played scoreless hockey through 60 minutes, then engaged in five overtime periods before rookie Red Wing "Mud" Bruneteau fired a 25-footer that beat Maroons goalie Lorne Chabot. The game ended at 2:25 a.m., after 176 minutes and 30 seconds of hockey.

Norm Smith, the winning goalie, who stopped 91 shots in that game, came back in game two to record a second straight shutout. His performances gave the Red Wings a huge lift, and they went on to whip Toronto in the final series to capture the Stanley Cup. Smith told the media: "I went to a pub in Montreal after the longest game and had a couple of beers. Then I staggered and almost fell down. People thought I was drunk but I was simply too exhausted to stand up."

Was the longest game his favourite hockey memory?

"It sure was. But the most bizarre memory I have of hockey was playing in Quebec. There were holes in the arena roof and flocks of pigeons would fly in to keep warm. They'd rest in the rafters right over my head. It's hard to concentrate on the game when you know you're going to be bombarded with pigeon poop at any moment. And the fans didn't help. They'd throw peanuts on the ice in front of me. The pigeons would swoop down, grab the peanuts, and return to the rafters. The peanuts kept them all at my end of the rink. That's why some of the NHL goalies wore caps on their heads in Quebec. Maybe we should have brought umbrellas, too."

The Red Wings went on to defeat Toronto in the 1936 finals, three games to one, and skated off with the Stanley Cup.

Thanks largely to Smith, who won the Vezina Trophy that season, the Red Wings repeated as league champions in 1936–37. In the playoffs that spring, Smith suffered an elbow injury in game three against the Canadiens that sent him to the sidelines. He came back for game five and was the winning goalie in a game that required 52 minutes of overtime.

In the finals against the Rangers, his sore elbow acted up, keeping him on the sidelines. Rookie netminder Earl Robertson took over and played a starring role as the Red Wings won their second straight Stanley Cup.

The Wings slipped badly the following year, and Jack Adams threatened a wholesale shakeup. Smith took much of the blame when the team missed the playoffs and fell into the basement.

Smith played just four games for Detroit in 1938–39, then bolted from the team after a game in New York. Adams suspended him and quickly made a deal with Boston, acquiring veteran Tiny Thompson. Smith's Red Wing career was apparently over.

Five seasons passed and, desperate for goaltending help during the war, Adams called Smith and invited him back. But his skills had eroded. He played a mere five games in 1943–44 and one more the following season. His NHL career wasn't long—only 198 games. But he won a Vezina Trophy and two Stanley Cups. And he'll always be remembered as the winning goalie in the longest game ever played.

Detroit defenceman Bucko McDonald was a double winner in that 1936 game.

Before the first game, Detroit's bashing defenceman was approached by a Red Wing fan who promised him five dollars for every Maroon he bodychecked to the ice during the match.

During the marathon, McDonald was at his bodychecking best. He flattened 37 Maroons during the equivalent of three normal games. In the stands, the gleeful fan kept score and was outside the dressing room with $185 in "hit" money when Bucko emerged.

Bucko thanked the fan, pocketed the cash, and went looking for a restaurant.

"Where am I going to find a place open at this hour?" he groaned. "It's after 3 a.m. and all I had for my pre-game meal was a boiled egg and dish of ice cream."

A similar marathon, one that stretched well into the wee, small hours, had been played in Toronto three seasons earlier.

On April 1, 1933, Maple Leaf Gardens was filled to capacity for the fifth and deciding game of a semifinal series between the Bruins and the Leafs. Some standing-room fans brought folding camp chairs and soft drink boxes to stand on—anything to elevate them a few inches in order to see over the heads of others and watch the thrilling action below.

At the end of what would be an amazing marathon match, the longest game (to that point) in hockey history, none of the attendees complained they hadn't got their money's worth. They had just witnessed a playoff game like no other.

At exactly 8:30 p.m., referees Daigneault and Cleghorn dropped the puck for the opening faceoff. At 1:48 the following morning, in the sixth period of overtime, the fans rocked Leaf owner Conn Smythe's new ice palace with a roar of appreciation as Ken Doraty, so small he'd never seen a parade, took a pass from six-foot, one-inch Andy Blair and whipped the puck past Boston goaltender Tiny Thompson for the only goal of the game. Until that moment, Thompson had been unbeatable and had faced 114 shots. His counterpart, Lorne Chabot in the Toronto goal, had been just as stingy and had faced 93 shots.

Blair and Doraty were two unlikely heroes. Doraty, one of the smallest players in hockey at 124 pounds, had recently been called up from Syracuse. In a previous trial with Chicago, he played 18 NHL games—without scoring a point! He was bluntly told he lacked endurance and simply wouldn't make the grade in the NHL. "Why didn't you become a jockey?" someone once asked him.

Blair, it was reported, was near the end of his career, although he would last another four seasons.

For 164 minutes and 46 seconds, the teams battled each other into a state of exhaustion. By the fifth overtime of the scoreless tie, they were mentally and physically drained. After the fifth overtime period, some players wanted to stop. But a conference with NHL President Frank Calder resulted in the decree: "Play to a finish!"

It had been suggested that a coin toss decide the outcome. Others said, "Play without goalies." Again, Calder made the call: "Play to a finish!"

"Good decision!" spat veteran Leaf Baldy Cotton. "Now let's go back out there and beat their sorry asses."

The goat of the contest turned out to be Bruin immortal Eddie Shore, the highest-paid and most feared defenceman in hockey. Blair intercepted Shore's cross-ice pass in the sixth overtime. Blair threw a quick pass to Doraty, who took a couple of choppy strides toward Thompson, fired the puck, and scored! The game had required 104:46 minutes of overtime play.

Hats flew out on the ice. Programs fluttered down. The crowd was delirious with delight. Before his mates could leap on Doraty's fragile frame, he dove into the net and retrieved the puck, a souvenir of the greatest athletic feat he would ever perform. His mates hugged and kissed him and dragged him back to the bench. Baldy Cotton skated around the ice kicking hats into the air. He fell down, got up, and did an Irish jig. He pulled a battered derby over his head and made comical faces at the fans.

Harold Ballard, just back from Europe, where he mismanaged a team called the Sea Fleas to a 2–1 loss to an American team in the World Hockey Championships and was thrown in jail in Paris after he slugged a policeman in a post-game brawl, blamed poor ice for the marathon game. The future owner of the Leafs said, "They couldn't resurface the ice properly in that era, so in the overtime periods the players were skating in slush up to their garter belts."

Boston coach Art Ross took the devastating loss like a champion. He embraced Leaf defenceman King Clancy and planted a kiss on the Irishman's cheek. Earlier in the season, during a dispute in Boston, a snarling Ross tried to plant another kind of kiss on Clancy—using his knuckles.

Doraty had no time to celebrate his feat. After the game, the Leafs rushed to board a special train that took them to New York and the first game of the final series, scheduled for the following night. The tight schedule was grossly unfair to the Leafs. They arrived late in the afternoon of the opener and, staggering with fatigue, were completely outclassed by the Rangers and lost by a 5–1 score. In game two, Doraty scored the lone Toronto goal in a 3–1 Ranger victory. The pocket-sized puckster collected two more goals in game three, won by the Leafs, 3–2. Bill Cook scored the only goal in game four—an overtime marker with two Leaf players in the penalty box—and the Rangers captured the Stanley Cup.

The two longest playoff games of the modern era took place in May 2000 and April 2003. On May 4, 2000, Philadelphia edged Pittsburgh 2–1 on Keith Primeau's goal in the fifth overtime period, after 92 minutes and one second of extra time. On April 24, 2003, Anaheim defeated Dallas 4–3 on Petr Sykora's goal at 80:48 of overtime — just after the teams took the ice for the fifth extra session.

Mel Hill Earns a Nickname

In the mid-1930s, Melvin Hill, a skinny right winger from Glenboro, Manitoba, was told he didn't have much future in hockey. "At 140 pounds, you don't have enough beef to make it to the NHL," the New York Rangers told him. "And your on-ice skills are strictly minor league."

Little Melvin was crushed at the Rangers' blunt appraisal.

"I'll be back," he told the Rangers' manager. "You'll be sorry you rejected me."

Hill played senior hockey in Sudbury for the next two seasons, and by 1938 he was back, 35 pounds heavier, fighting for an NHL job. He caught on as a regular—not with the Rangers, but with the Boston Bruins. But even though he was in the NHL, earning about $3,000, he was not a first-line player and his future was still uncertain. He managed to score 10 goals in his first full season and with famous teammates like Eddie Shore, Dit Clapper, Bill Cowley, and Milt Schmidt surrounding him, he felt like a sparrow nesting with eagles.

When the Bruins rolled into the 1938 playoffs, Hill desperately wanted to make some kind of mark. He wanted to keep that big-league paycheque coming in. When his Bruins met the Rangers in the '38 Cup semifinals, Hill thirsted for revenge against the club that had discarded him only a few years earlier. In the opener, Hill scored a dramatic overtime goal to finish off a six-period marathon match. In game two, Hill scored again in overtime to give the Bruins a 2–0 lead in the series. Boston won game three in regulation time and grabbed a commanding 3–0 lead in the series. But the desperate Rangers fought back with three straight victories to force a seventh and deciding game, the match to be played at the Boston Garden.

Game seven became a tight-checking, low-scoring affair, and produced the most thrilling hockey of the series. The score was tied 1–1 at the end of 60 minutes and the game went into overtime. That's when every Bruin fan in the building kept a close eye on Hill, praying he could strike one more time with his overtime magic.

The first two overtime periods were scoreless. Late in the third extra frame, Hill took a pass from Bill Cowley and slapped the puck past Ranger goalie Dave Kerr. Incredibly, he had done it again. His third overtime goal of the series had captured the game and the series. By the following day, reporters everywhere were referring to unheralded John Melvin Hill, the little winger from Glenboro, Manitoba, as Mel "Sudden Death" Hill, scoring hero of the Stanley Cup playoffs. The nickname would stick and be his moniker for the remainder of his life.

Hill's Bruins went on to win the Stanley Cup that year, defeating Toronto four games to one in the finals. When the Stanley Cup was presented to the Bruins at the Boston Garden, the fans roared first for Eddie Shore, who had played superbly on defence despite a broken nose and a black eye suffered in a one-sided fight with Ranger heavyweight Muzz Patrick in the semifinals. When Shore skated off the ice, the second-loudest ovation went to Melvin Hill, who was already counting on the bonus money he'd receive: $2,000 for the Stanley Cup win and a special bonus of $1,000 for his three overtime goals. This bonus money equalled his regular-season earnings of $3,000. Not only did Hill gain revenge on the Rangers, but he doubled his income in the process.

Boston ace Milt Schmidt was still a teenager that season and has often said that Hill's playoff heroics, and Eddie Shore's stellar performances, were among his favourite hockey memories. "After we won the Cup, I was amazed to see Shore leave the ice before the Cup was presented and before the fans could give him a proper, well-deserved ovation.

"Brian, the ovation for Eddie that night was incredible. I'll never forget it. Shore skated off right after the victory—don't ask me why—and the fans were stunned. Maybe Eddie had a premonition the Bruins were going to trade him a year later. I don't know. He was a very funny guy and did some strange things.

"Anyway, the Boston fans wouldn't let NHL president Frank Calder present the Stanley Cup until Shore could be found. I mean, Shore was our team leader. He was hockey's answer to Babe Ruth. He should have been there—front and centre.

"He was found in our dressing room with his equipment half off. I guess he could hear the fans chanting, 'We want Shore! We want Shore!' That convinced him to return, and when he skated back out, the ovation that man received was absolutely incredible. It was ear-shattering. I was only 19 years old and I had goose pimples breaking out all over my body. I couldn't believe the din. I wouldn't hear another ovation like that one until the Bruins held Bobby Orr Night at the Boston Garden on January 9, 1979. I figured the ovation for Orr was equal to or even louder and longer than the one they gave Shore 40 years earlier."

Shore may have been a hero in Boston, but he was not a popular player around the league.

Former referee and Stanley Cup trustee Cooper Smeaton called him a threat to the life of the other players in the league.

"He was a nasty guy, a madman. He almost killed Ace Bailey of the Leafs, ending the career of one of the best-liked players in the game. I threw him out of a game one night when he pushed me around. But his manager, Art Ross, protested my decision, and the governors sided with Ross because Shore sold tickets. He was a drawing card. I resigned on the spot and it took a lot of persuasion from the governors to get me to come back."

Forgive me if I stretch this story out with a few words about one of my boyhood heroes—Boston star Bill Cowley.

Cowley, I maintain, was more responsible for Mel Hill's nickname than anyone else. He was the player who assisted on all three of Hill's famous overtime goals, and he was one of Boston's biggest bargains. In 1935, he was drafted from the defunct St. Louis Eagles for $2,250. While not fast, Cowley was an incredible playmaker.

The record that Cowley was proudest of was set during the 1943-44 season.

He was having one of his most productive seasons and jumped ahead of everybody in the scoring race, collecting 53 points by January 7, 1944. Then a collision with a rival player left him with a separated shoulder. The injury kept him out of the lineup for a month. He was back on the ice by mid-February, but was sidelined again with another injury, this time to his knee.

That season, in just 36 games, he finished up with 71 points, an average of 1.97 points per game. This record stood for more than 38 years. Finally, in 1981-82, Wayne Gretzky, the NHL's all-time points leader, scored a record 212 points, averaging 2.65 points per game. Since then, only two players have consistently averaged more than two points per game in a season—Gretzky and Mario Lemieux. Gretsky is the current record holder with a 2.77 average set in 1983-84. For Cowley to remain third on the list, after more than 60 years—is truly remarkable.

Cowley was one of the NHL's all time great playmakers. He was a two-time Hart Trophy winner and was inducted into the Hockey Hall of Fame in 1968.

I particularly admired Cowley for a little known but remarkable display of sportsmanship he showed during the 1942-43 season. During the season, he was on track to break his own record for most assists in a season (45) set in 1941. After a game between Boston and the Rangers one night, Cowley sent a letter to NHL President Red Dutton, asking Dutton to erase an assist he had been given, one he felt he had not earned.

Dutton, a former player himself, had never heard of a player asking to have a point deducted from his scoring record. But he granted Cowley's request. A perfect ending to the story would have seen Cowley win the Art

Ross Trophy as scoring champion. Alas, he finished second, one point back of Chicago's Max Bentley. Also, the point he had deducted cost him a new record for assists. He wound up tying his previous league mark of 45. And when he retired in 1947, his career total of 548 points was just one point less than the number of games he'd played—549.

Now you know why Bill Cowley was one of my hockey heroes.

Broda Was a Bargain

In the spring of 1936, Toronto Maple Leaf owner Conn Smythe watched in horror as his goalie, George Hainsworth, gave up nine goals to the Red Wings in a playoff game played at the Detroit Olympia. "I've got to find a replacement for old George," Smythe muttered angrily.

Smythe stayed in Detroit to scout Earl Robertson, a Detroit netminding prospect with a "can't-miss" reputation. But it wasn't Robertson who impressed Smythe. In a minor-league game the following day, a burly goalie on the opposing team—a 21-year-old netminder from Brandon, Manitoba, named Walter "Turk" Broda—left Smythe drooling. Broda, like Robertson, was owned by the Red Wings but was lightly regarded. The youngster wondered if he'd ever get a chance to wear a big-league uniform.

Detroit manager Jack Adams said he'd be happy to part with Broda or Robertson for the sum of $8,000. If Smythe couldn't see that Robertson was a much better prospect than the kid from Brandon, perhaps he should consider getting a white cane to go with his white spats. Ignoring Adams's sharp tongue, Smythe anted up for the chubby Broda and Adams happily pocketed the money. Not for a second did he believe Smythe had just bought himself a future Hall of Famer.

At first, Smythe's cronies were skeptical of his purchase. One of them said: "Broda's a yappy guy and he's got the appetite of a horse. You pay him a big-league salary, he'll eat himself out of the league in no time."

Smythe smiled and said, "Gentlemen, he's only 21. Let's just wait and see."

It didn't take long for the rotund Broda to establish himself as one of the game's best puck stoppers. At the same time, he became one of hockey's most popular players. From 1936 to 1952, he played in 628 games for the Leafs and recorded 62 shutouts. He played in 101 Stanley Cup playoff games, a record at the time, and chalked up 13 playoff shutouts, another record. He won the Vezina Trophy twice, with a 2.06 average in 1940–41 and a 2.38 average in 1947–48. His 1948 Vezina prevented Montreal's Bill Durnan from capturing the trophy seven times in a row.

Broda led the Leafs to five Stanley Cups, including four in five years in the late 1940s. His work in the playoffs was often spectacular, and even today he is named by old-timers as one of hockey's greatest "money" goaltenders.

In the 1949 Stanley Cup final series against Detroit, Broda allowed just five goals in four games as the Leafs swept the Red Wings aside for their third straight Cup triumph. How often Adams must have rued the day he let Broda go.

In 1951, at age 37, he allowed just nine goals in eight games as Toronto won the Cup again, this time on Bill Barilko's memorable overtime goal against Montreal. "We couldn't beat the guy," Rocket Richard fumed. "We had some great scorers but we couldn't put the puck behind him."

Smythe held a night for Broda on December 22, 1951. Only one other Leaf—King Clancy—had been honoured in such a manner. It was Broda's last season. He played in only one game during the regular season, but after Al Rollins lost the opening game of the playoff series with Detroit, Turk got the call. In game two, he played brilliantly, only to lose 1–0 in his 100th playoff start. He started again in game three against the Wings and was shelled 6–2. Rollins finished up as the Leafs bowed out in four games.

Leaf owner Conn Smythe once said, "If we had to play one game with everything at stake, Turk Broda would be my choice as goaltender. Acquiring Broda was one of the best moves I ever made in hockey."

"No More Beer, Alfie, You're Playing Tonight"

Seventy years ago, a beer-drinking goalie and a coach who knew more about baseball than hockey were key players in Chicago's bid for a Stanley Cup. The goalie was a fill-in, Alfie Moore, who turned in a sterling "one night only" performance for the Chicago Blackhawks in their 1938 bid for the Cup. The coach was Bill Stewart, a baseball umpire and referee, a highly unlikely choice to oversee an NHL club.

After winning only 14 of 48 regular-season games under rookie coach Stewart, the Blackhawks crawled into the playoffs just two points ahead of last-place Detroit.

Rival managers had snickered when Chicago owner Frederic McLaughlin hired Stewart to manage and coach his Blackhawks. "He never coached or managed a hockey team anywhere," chuckled one. "He was merely a referee."

"He never played hockey," snorted another. "He's a baseball guy. McLaughlin must be losing his marbles."

But somehow Stewart steered a team with a record eight American-born players, a team that scored fewer than a hundred regular-season goals, into the 1938 playoffs. Bolstered by the splendid goaltending of Mike Karakas, the Hawks caught fire in the post-season and pulled off two upsets, first against the Montreal Canadiens and then over the New York Americans. To their amazement, they had reached the Stanley Cup finals against the powerful Toronto Maple Leafs.

But not all of the Hawks were prepared for the finals. Star goaltender Karakas was nursing a broken toe and couldn't slip his swollen foot into his skate prior to the first game in Toronto. "You'd better find a substitute goalie," he told Stewart.

But where to find a quality goaltender at the last minute? Stewart knew that Ranger goalie Dave Kerr was in Toronto and planned to attend the game that night, but Leaf owner Conn Smythe scoffed at Stewart's request to use him. "Not him," said Smythe. "Kerr's too good. But I'll let you have one of my minor-league goalies—Alfie Moore. If you can find him, that is."

Stewart sent a couple of his players in a search for Moore. They found him drinking beer in his favourite tavern. Moore greeted them warmly. "You fellows got an extra ticket for the game tonight?" he asked.

"You won't need a ticket, Alfie," they replied. "Come with us. You're going to be *in* the game, not at it."

In the Chicago dressing room, after downing several cups of black coffee, Moore suited up as the replacement for Karakas. In the opening minutes of play it appeared to have been a huge mistake to let him play. The first shot he faced ripped into his net and the Leafs took a 1–0 lead.

But Moore pulled himself together and was the picture of confidence and composure throughout the rest of the match. He skated off triumphantly with a 3–1 victory amid a lot of back-slapping from his new teammates. Moore couldn't resist thumbing his nose at Leaf owner Conn Smythe en route to the dressing room.

But Smythe got even prior to game two. He convinced the league president, Frank Calder, to declare Moore ineligible for the rest of the series. "He's our property, not theirs," Smythe snarled. "We're not giving him a second chance to make us look bad."

Goalie Paul Goodman, an obscure minor leaguer with no NHL experience, filled in for Karakas—and Moore—in game two at Toronto and suffered a 5–1 defeat. Goodman was very nervous, and the Hawks' stunning playoff run appeared to be over.

Then came word that Mike Karakas, having arranged for a shoemaker to outfit him with a specially constructed skate to protect his broken toe, would return for the rest of the series. Karakas played a starring role in the Hawks' next game on home ice, a 2–1 victory, and followed up with a solid performance in game four. The Hawks won that game 4–1, and the Stanley Cup was theirs.

Chicago's stunning Stanley Cup victory of 1938 has often been called the greatest upset in NHL history. Chicago's 14–25–9 regular-season record remains the worst ever for a Cup champion.

As for Alfie Moore, when asked by Bill Stewart what he thought his one-game victory was worth in monetary terms, Moore replied, "I dunno, Bill. How about paying me $150?" Stewart pulled out a roll of bills and peeled off $300. Later, Stewart made sure that Moore received a gold watch and that his name was engraved on the Stanley Cup. Moore said later, "Hockey's a funny game. I played in only 21 NHL games in my entire career, and because I played in one game with Chicago I get to see my name on the Stanley Cup. That's unbelievable.

"But I never got to drink from the Cup," he adds. "When we won it in Chicago, it was nowhere to be found. Some of my new teammates were really upset about that."

Carl Voss, who scored the series-winning goal for Chicago, was furious when he learned he wouldn't get to hold the Stanley Cup in the post-season celebration.

"Where is it?" he demanded. "I want to sip some Champagne from it."

"Oh, it's back in Toronto," someone explained. "Everybody assumed there'd be another game in the series. Nobody believed you'd knock the Leafs off in four games."

Voss broke out laughing. "Hell, we didn't believe it either," he said.

III. Champions of the Original Six Era

Adams Suspended After Rink Chase

Detroit Red Wing manager Jack Adams, like many a hockey manager, was loved by some and reviled by others. But even those who disliked the man grudgingly admit that the dictatorial old buzzard deserves a place in the Hockey Hall of Fame, for he moulded championship teams and created a remarkable niche in Stanley Cup history.

After joining Detroit as manager-coach in 1927, following a long playing career, he guided his teams to seven Stanley Cups and 12 league titles. From 1949 to 1955, his Detroit Red Wings achieved success that surpassed even baseball's New York Yankees in their heyday. Detroit finished in first place for seven consecutive seasons. And his ace right winger, Gordie Howe, was the NHL's leading scorer in four of them.

Adams often boasted: "Our 1951–52 team that won the playoffs in eight straight games over Toronto and Montreal was the greatest hockey team ever assembled. We had Howe, Lindsay, Abel, and Sawchuk. Why, Sawchuk didn't allow a single goal on home ice in either of the two playoff rounds in '52. And we had a great supporting cast."

"Hockey's the greatest game there is," Adams once said. "It has to be, to survive the number of jerks that are in it."

Despite his nickname, "Jolly Jack" Adams could be a ruthless and controversial figure. He shunted Ted Lindsay, his great left winger, off to Chicago when Lindsay became president of a fledgling players' association. Adams detested unions and considered Lindsay's union ambitions to be treasonous. Adams rarely spoke to Lindsay in the last two seasons they were together.

Lindsay was never shy about rating Adams as a manager.

"He never deserved all the accolades he won," states Lindsay, still a firebrand at age 83. "I say Jack Adams was a lousy hockey man. I say he cheated me out of at least five and maybe as many as seven or eight Stanley Cups.

"After we won two Cups in a row in 1954 and '55, he traded nine players away from the Red Wings. Nine players! Why? We could have stayed on top. Instead, we went downhill from there.

"What really rankles is the trade he should have made but didn't. After we won in '55, the Canadiens wanted our goalie, Terry Sawchuk. We could have parted with Terry because we had Glenn Hall, a splendid young goaltender, waiting in the wings. And we could have acquired Doug Harvey, one of the greatest defencemen ever to play the game, in return for Sawchuk. Adams refused to make the deal, and the Habs went on to win five consecutive Stanley Cups with Harvey leading them every step of the way. He was the Bobby Orr of his era.

"Adams said he wouldn't make the trade because he didn't want to make Montreal stronger. Geez, they won the next five Cups. How much stronger could he have made them?"

But let's cut to the chase here—the famous chase around the ice Adams led at the end of the fourth game of the Cup finals in 1942.

The fiery manager made headlines by jumping onto the ice during the game against Toronto. Furious over the injustice of the penalty calls he witnessed, he bulled his way into an altercation between game officials and several players. It was charged (and denied by Adams) that he threw punches at referee Mel Harwood. Some reporters and columnists wrote scathing denunciations of Adams's behaviour and asked that he be suspended from hockey forever. When he threatened libel suits against them, many of the journalists hastily penned apologies.

Several years later, Adams told writer Trent Frayne in *Maclean's* magazine: "The fourth game in that '42 series was the bitterest of my career. We were leading the series 3–0 and leading in what should have been the final game with 15 minutes to play. Then we lost by a goal after some of the most incredible refereeing I've ever seen. When the fourth game ended, three of my players, Grosso, Wares and Abel, engaged referee Mel Harwood in a heated argument. I went skidding across the ice after them to pull my players away and was charged with belting the referee. Actually, I didn't get within ten feet of the guy, but the league president, Frank Calder, suspended me for the balance of the series and fined Wares and Grosso $100 each. Then Toronto came back to win the series, taking four games in a row. It was an incredible comeback, the first and only time that had ever happened. To me, the series seemed to be controlled by the Toronto newspapers and [Leaf owner] Conn Smythe. Their influence on Calder was, no doubt, my darkest moment in hockey."

Bob Davidson, who spent 44 years in the Toronto organization as a player and scout, played on the Leafs' Cup-winning team in 1942. He said there was some real motivation to win.

"After trailing Detroit 3–0 in the series, we were determined to win the next game. We had no idea we were about to make an astonishing comeback with four straight wins. Who would have believed that would happen? Coach Hap Day stunned the hockey world when he benched Gordie Drillon, our leading scorer, along with defenceman Bucko McDonald. Aside from some player changes, two things happened to get us in a winning mood before that fourth game in Detroit. First, Jack Adams, the Detroit manager, went on radio and said his team would wrap it up in the four games. He sounded pretty cocky, and it made us really mad. Then Hap Day read us a letter from a little girl in Toronto who said she'd be ashamed to go to school the next day if we lost four straight games in the finals. That inspired us to do our best.

"Even so, we fell behind 2–0 in the second period. Then I scored a goal that got us going and we won 4–3. We simply wouldn't be beaten. In the fifth game we walloped Detroit 9–3 and our goalie, Turk Broda, shut them out 3–0 in game six. What a crowd turned out for the deciding game back in

Toronto. Over 16,000 fans jammed Maple Leaf Gardens—a record for attendance. In the dressing room before game seven, owner Conn Smythe asked Sweeney Schriner, one of our veterans, 'Are you ready for this? Are we going to win tonight?' And Schriner told him, 'Don't worry, boss. You'll soon be riding in a Stanley Cup parade.' Then Schriner, who was born in Russia and emigrated to Canada with his family as an eight-year-old, led us to the Cup with a pair of goals in a 3–1 triumph.

"After we captured the Stanley Cup, captain Syl Apps and I went to visit the little girl who'd written the letter and told her how much she'd helped us."

Jack Adams had many bitter memories aside from that folderoo in '42. He believed that Frank Mahovlich, as a teenager in the early 1950s, reneged on a commitment to play for Detroit. He said, "Frank and his father certainly double-crossed our organization. We will not forget it. When a man's word is no good, he is no good."

He bristled at the roughhouse tactics of Rocket Richard and once called the Montreal superstar "a hatchetman who deliberately injures players. We will not stand for any more of his vicious play."

During his playing days, Adams scored 83 career goals. One of his markers stands out as one of the oddest in history. Playing for Vancouver in 1921, he accidentally scored a goal on his own netminder. And it counted! Somehow he was credited with the goal on the official score sheet. The goal vaulted him into fifth place in the league scoring race.

Some hockey people, then and now, speak highly of Adams. In 1966, he impressed enough of them to be named the first winner of the Lester Patrick Trophy for contributions to hockey in the United States.

Defenceman Larry Hillman, who played on six Stanley Cup teams during a nomadic career that took him to eight NHL cities and two markets in the WHA, credits Jack Adams for giving him his start in pro hockey.

"I was a rookie, an 18-year-old defenceman with the Red Wings, when Adams gave me a chance," Hillman recalls. "Heck, I only played in six regular-season games and three playoff games and I didn't collect a single point.

Then, suddenly, after nine games, I'm on the 1955 Cup-winning team—right there with Gordie and Ted and Terry. We beat Montreal in the seventh game 3–1 at the Olympia. That much success, coming so early, made my head spin. It was like a dream. I wasn't even old enough to vote. I had no idea there'd be five more Cups to follow, four with Toronto and another with Montreal."

"Was the Detroit Cup win your favourite?" I asked Hillman. "It was your first, after all."

"No, my favourite Cup win was with the Leafs in '67," he replied, but not before giving it a moment's thought. "That's because it was the last year of the old six-team league and because nobody gave the Leafs a chance to knock off both Chicago and Montreal. And I feel I contributed a lot to the success of that '67 team."

Barilko's Career Ends Tragically

Any list of Stanley Cup thrill-producers would contain names like Bob Nystrom, Bobby Orr, little Ken Doraty, Mud Bruneteau, Bobby Baun, Rocket Richard, Mario Lemieux, and Wayne Gretzky, all of whom seized the moment and scored dramatic playoff goals that have been, and will be, talked about for decades.

High on any honour roll of NHL performers who've achieved instant-hero status is the name William "Bashin' Bill" Barilko. Barilko's golden moment in the Stanley Cup playoffs thrilled a full house at Maple Leaf Gardens on April 21, 1951. His Cup-winning blast occurred in sudden-death overtime against the Montreal Canadiens.

After 2:53 of extra time in game five of the finals, Barilko dashed boldly in from his defence position, and, while falling through the air, whacked the puck into the Montreal goal. Barilko crashed to the ice as the rubber whizzed past Gerry McNeil, the Habs' startled netminder.

While McNeil turned in dismay to see the red light flash, Barilko and his mates began celebrating their fourth Cup victory in five years. The Barilko goal ended a five-game final series that required overtime in every game before it was settled.

After mobbing their grinning teammate, the Leafs hoisted Barilko to their shoulders. He was awarded a thunderous standing ovation from the Toronto faithful. Owner Conn Smythe and coach Joe Primeau skidded across the ice to pump his hand. Later, Bill's mother, Faye, using a soup spoon, helped hockey's newest celebrity sip Champagne from the bowl of the Stanley Cup. This beaming woman had fled Russia in 1924 to begin a new life in Timmins, Ontario. Losing her husband in 1946 had been a terrible blow, but on this night she was ecstatic, the proudest mother in Canada. To think that her 24-year-old son, so handsome, so talented, was the object of everyone's attention left her all but speechless.

But wait! Barilko might never have been a playoff hero had it not been for a last-minute goal in regulation time that tied the score. With Montreal leading by a 2–1 count and Gerry McNeil performing miracles in goal, Primeau pulled his goalie and sent out six attackers. Ted Kennedy beat Elmer Lach on the faceoff, passed the puck to Max Bentley, who skimmed a shot through the crease. Sid Smith tapped it over to Tod Sloan, who slipped it into the open corner. There were just 32 seconds left on the clock.

Barilko's goal made him a national hero. Mrs. Barilko's shriek of delight was heard a moment later. But her joy would be short-lived. A few weeks later, back home in Timmins, she would be found nursing a broken heart.

Against his mother's wishes, son Bill flew off with his dentist friend Henry Hudson, pilot of a Fairchild 24. Hudson took Barilko on a fly-in fishing trip to some northern lakes and rivers. Later, through her tears, his mother would say, "Oh, I made such a terrible mistake, letting him go, not kissing him goodbye, being angry with him for leaving, not telling him I loved him. I begged him not to go on a Friday. Fridays are bad luck. I lost my husband on a Friday."

Hall of Fame defenceman Allan Stanley was supposed to be on the flight with Barilko. "I was all set to go," Stanley told me. "But there was some kind of mix-up. Henry and Bill decided to take Henry's brother Lou instead. But there was a dead calm on the water that morning and the plane had trouble taking off. Too much weight. So they dropped Lou off. With one less passenger, the plane made it safely into the air.

"On Monday morning I showed up for my dental appointment and the nurse told me, 'Henry's not back yet.' That's when we began to worry that something had gone wrong."

Barilko and Hudson flew 300 miles north to the rivers that flow into James Bay, where the fishing was superb. Two days later, with the plane's pontoons loaded with fish, they started back. But somewhere along the way, their plane went down without a trace.

A massive search was organized. Hundreds of private planes and at least 17 aircraft from the Royal Canadian Air Force criss-crossed thousands of acres of dense bush. Day after day, the flights took off. None reported any sightings. Months went by, and then years, and the disappearance of the popular hockey star and his friend remained a baffling mystery.

Then, in 1962, helicopter pilot Garry Fields spotted the reflection of the sun glinting on a piece of metal buried in the deep bush about 50 miles north of Timmins. He marked the spot with some toilet tissue thrown into the tree branches. A few hours later he led a search party into the area and located the missing aircraft. The skeletal remains of Barilko and his pilot friend were found inside.

"The plane's wings snapped off when it crashed into the tall spruce trees," Fields would report. "The branches folded back when the fuselage drove deep into the woods and buried itself in the forest floor. Then the branches folded over the wreckage. That's why it was so difficult to spot from the air."

The mystery of the missing Stanley Cup hero had finally been solved.

The Octopus Tossers

In the spring of 1952, the mighty Detroit Red Wings—the Wings of Howe, Lindsay, Abel, and Sawchuk—were sailing undefeated through the Stanley Cup playoffs. They swept through the semifinal series against Toronto without tasting defeat, and after three more victories over Montreal in the final series, they were poised to win the Stanley Cup with a perfect playoff record. And they would do it on home ice, too, much to the delight of their fans.

Two rabid Detroit fans attending the game were the Cusimano brothers, Jerry and Pete. Their affection for the Red Wings took an unusual twist prior to the final game. Jerry Cusimano suggested to his brother that they all but assure a Detroit win in the final match by "bringing a little good luck to the team."

"How'll we do that?" Pete asked.

"We're in the fish business, aren't we? We'll go to the game and we'll toss an octopus on the ice. An octopus has eight tentacles. It'll be a symbol of eight straight victories for the Red Wings. What do you say?"

"I say it's a great idea," Pete answered, his face lighting up.

So, on April 15, 1952, during the final game of the playoffs, Jerry Cusimano stood up and heaved a three-pound, partially boiled octopus—cooked just enough to bring out the pink colour—onto the ice at the Detroit Olympia.

Splat!

"You should have seen referee Frank Udvari jump when that octopus landed nearby," Pete says. "His face turned white and he backed away from it like it was a hand grenade. Then, when he moved in close and took a whiff, he wouldn't go near the thing. Those things really stink. Finally, a rink attendant came out with a shovel and carried it away.

"Detroit won the game and the Stanley Cup that night. Final score was 3–0. Sawchuk was cheered to the rafters because it was his second straight shutout, and in the four games he allowed just two Montreal goals. But we figured our octopus was a key to the victory. So we began doing it every year in the playoffs. It became a ritual, something the fans looked forward to."

"Did you ever hit anyone with one of those smelly things?" someone asks.

"We tried to," Pete Cusimano confesses. "Ted Kennedy of the Leafs got us mad one year and one of us took dead aim at him. But we hit his linemate, Vic Lynn, by mistake—right in the kisser. Scared the hell out of him. Geez, he was mad, glaring up at the crowd, trying to spot us."

Over the last half-century, many fans have followed the Cusimanos' lead. But none have gained as much notoriety as the brothers who originated the bizarre custom.

On TV recently, a standup comedian told his audience, "I took my mother-in-law to a big sporting event at the Joe Louis Arena one night. Suddenly, she emulated the Cusimanos by hauling an octopus out of a bag and hurling it onto the ice. I said, 'Mom. You just scared the crap out of Katarina Witt.' "

Five in a Row Is Fantastic

The 1959–60 season was another banner year for the Montreal Canadiens. The regular schedule ended with Montreal in first place with 40 wins and 92 points—13 points more than second-place Toronto. The other two clubs to fight their way into the post-season, third-place Chicago and fourth-place Detroit, played under .500 and managed only 69 and 65 points respectively.

Now the Habs set out to capture an unprecedented fifth consecutive Stanley Cup. It would be a monumental accomplishment. The Montreal roster was basically the same as the one that had started the dynasty in 1955–56. Still with the club were future Hall of Famers Jacques Plante, Doug Harvey, Tom Johnson, Maurice and Henri Richard, Boom Boom Geoffrion, Dickie Moore, and Jean Beliveau.

But many of these heroes were getting on in years, and other teams were getting stronger. There were fears that Chicago, with rising stars Bobby Hull and Stan Mikita up front and backed by Glenn Hall's masterful goaltending, would end the Canadiens' playoff streak in the opening round.

But the Habs handled the Hawks easily, sweeping the series in four straight games and outscoring their opponents 14–6.

Now Toe Blake's men braced themselves for the finals against Toronto. New coach Punch Imlach was attempting to build a dynasty of his own with the Leafs, a team that gained strength and confidence as the season wound down.

Imlach showed up for the first game at the Forum with several four-leaf clovers pinned to his clothes. But the foliage brought him no luck once the puck was dropped. The Habs banged in three goals before the 12-minute mark and coasted to a 4–2 victory.

In game two, Moore and Beliveau scored in the first six minutes of play. The Leafs got one back in the third period, but they couldn't stick the puck past Plante for the equalizer. Montreal 2, Toronto 1.

Game three in Toronto resulted in an easy 5–2 win for Montreal, high-lighted by the goaltending wizardry of Jacques Plante and Rocket Richard's first goal of the 1960 playoffs. It was Richard's 82nd playoff goal, the most in NHL history. It would also prove to be the final goal of his illustrious career. In time, Wayne Gretzky and others would surpass his playoff goal record, Gretzky finishing with 122.

After 18 seasons, Richard must have had retirement in mind when he skated in to retrieve the history-making puck. Five months, later he would attend Montreal's fall training camp, score four or five goals in one of the early scrimmages, then walk into Frank Selke's office to announce that he would play no more.

In game four, another fast start by Montreal left the Leafs frustrated and discouraged. Beliveau and Harvey scored goals 18 seconds apart in the first 10 minutes and Jacques Plante recorded the shutout in a 4–0 triumph.

The jubilant Canadiens had swept to their fifth consecutive Cup triumph— with no end in sight for their dynasty.

While the Habs drank from the Cup, fans predicted their winning streak would stretch into six, seven, even 10 straight championships. At the time, there was no inkling that the early '60s would belong to the Blackhawks and the Leafs.

By winning in the minimum number of games, the Canadiens equalled a record set by the Detroit Red Wings in the 1952 playoffs.

There was a modest victory celebration following the final game. Perhaps Doug Harvey said it for all the players when he told reporters, "When you win eight straight games in the playoffs and you win five Cups in a row, there's not a whole lot to get excited about."

"Harvey was the best defenceman of our day," said Leaf captain George Armstrong. "Playing against him was like playing against Wayne Gretzky or Bobby Orr. Those kind of players always find a way to beat you."

Howie Meeker, who played against Harvey for several seasons, recalled the defenceman's ability to control a game. "The tough son of a gun always came out of nowhere to become the biggest thorn in our side. He was like Bobby Orr, only a shade slower. You knew what he was doing; you could see him do it. But you couldn't do much about it."

When he broke in with Montreal in 1947–48, fans would have scoffed if they'd been told this lackadaisical rookie would lead the Canadiens to half a dozen Stanley Cups. And capture seven Norris Trophies as the NHL's top defenceman. Or play 20 NHL seasons and be named a First Team All-Star 10 times.

They didn't see his talent at first, only his lack of it. They booed him when they first saw him play. He looked so nonchalant, so hesitant with the puck in the Montreal zone. And yet, despite his imperfections, he never seemed to cough up the puck or make a major mistake. And he controlled the tempo of the game like no other player in history. In time, everyone relaxed. They began to appreciate his novel approach and the plaudits began to pour in. He shrugged them off. Despite all the team and personal accomplishments that followed, Harvey was seldom happy. He was a troubled man, a drinking man who often raged against the hockey establishment. "I didn't drink," he'd protest, winking, "unless I was real thirsty."

He snarled at the mention of hockey pioneers like Frank Selke and Conn Smythe. When the Hall of Fame selection committee ignored Harvey in 1972, the year they bent the rules to usher in Gordie Howe and Jean Beliveau a couple of years early, he blamed Selke and Smythe. "They don't want me in there because I've been known to hoist a few," he said. "And they've never forgiven me for helping to form a players' association. Did they blackball me for that? Sure they did."

The Hall of Fame welcomed Harvey the following year but, still angry, he ignored the honour. "I'll be out fishing that day," he said, and he kept his word.

After helping the Habs win five consecutive Cups, Harvey was traded to the Rangers in 1961 even though he had just been named a First Team All-Star and awarded the Norris Trophy. "That was my punishment," he said bitterly, "for helping Ted Lindsay and others try to organize the player's association a few years earlier.

"I would have been traded long before that, but we kept winning all those Cups. Selke didn't dare get rid of me. He knew the fans would have rioted."

I saw Harvey perform on the baseball diamond long before I saw him on skates. It was in Ottawa in the late '40s. I remember him as an outstanding ball player. He batted .351 with the Class C Ottawa Nationals one season. I had heard he was headed for a major league career with the Boston Braves. But Harvey's first love was always hockey. He was also a brilliant football player and just missed playing on a Grey Cup winner in 1944. It was said he could punt a football 65 yards. He quit football to join the Royal Canadian Navy, where he turned to boxing and won the navy heavyweight championship.

Harvey joined the Canadiens in 1947–48 and quickly proved himself the equal of any of hockey's greatest defencemen. When the Canadiens required a captain to replace Butch Bouchard in 1956, the players were quietly urged to vote for Maurice Richard and ignore Harvey, despite his obvious leadership qualities.

With the Rangers, as player-coach, he led the team into the playoffs for the first time since 1958, but he gave up the coaching job after one season. "I liked the playing part better," he said. "You know, being with the boys, tossing back a few after the game. Having fun. I never really liked coaching that much."

He played briefly with the Red Wings in 1966–67 and joined the St. Louis Blues for the playoffs in 1968. His final season was in 1968–69, when he gave the Blues the best a 45-year-old could offer.

When he died of cirrhosis of the liver on a chilly December day in 1989, hockey men were quick to mourn the passing of Doug Harvey.

"When I joined Montreal," said Jean Beliveau, "he was the best defenceman I'd ever seen."

"I feel very sad," said Maurice Richard. "We had a lot of fun together. Doug was great, always willing to help."

If Harvey marched to a different drumbeat, so did goaltender Jacques Plante.

It was during the dynasty years that Plante became the premier netminder in hockey—and the most controversial. He revolutionized the game and changed the art of netminding for the better. He's best remembered for becoming the first goaltender in modern-day hockey to don the face mask (on November 1, 1959, and against coach Toe Blake's wishes), but perhaps an even greater gift to the game was his insistence that goalies could contribute more—by roaming from their nets, by passing pucks to teammates, by trapping loose pucks in back of the goal, by shouting instructions to forwards and defencemen. He may have driven Blake and the fans wild with his eccentricities, but he captured seven Vezina Trophies and six Stanley Cups. He must have been doing something right. I interviewed him often on television and marvelled at his ability to analyze the game.

He revealed he was paid to play as a 15-year-old—in Shawinigan Falls, Quebec. "I asked my coach if he had some money for me," he recalled. "He said he'd give me fifty cents. But I had to promise not to tell the other players on the team."

The famous Soviet coach Anatoli Tarasov once said, "Plante was the greatest goalie I ever saw."

Plante died in Sierre, Switzerland, in 1986.

Beliveau told me, "I went to the funeral and discovered that he had left behind some wonderful poems he had written. His widow donated them to the National Archives in Ottawa."

The Ugly Forum Riot

"Can you imagine sports fans in any other city, in any other sport, rioting in the streets because one of their team's best players was suspended? Of course not. It just wouldn't happen. But it happened in Montreal—on St. Patrick's Day, 1955.

"It wasn't a playoff game, but it took place on the eve of the playoffs, had a huge impact on the playoff race like no other. It followed a suspension. And it had no ending."

Those words, spoken by my *Hockey Night in Canada* colleague Dick Irvin, brought back memories of the ugly riot at the Montreal Forum over half a century ago.

NHL president Clarence Campbell had suspended Montreal superstar Rocket Richard after a March 13 game in Boston. Richard had gone wild, chopping the Bruins' Hal Laycoe with his stick and then punching linesman Cliff Thompson, who tried to intervene. Richard's suspension for the final three games of the season and the entire playoffs triggered a furious, frightening reaction from his legion of fans. Campbell was lucky to escape without serious injury and even his life.

Dick and I were college kids back then, he at McGill, I at St. Lawrence University in Canton, New York, and both of us will forever remember the shock we felt as events unfolded four nights later at the Forum. The visitors were the Detroit Red Wings. The explosions of anger and frustration could not be controlled. Campbell was physically assaulted, a tear gas bomb exploded, the game was halted (it was never finished), and the fans were ordered to vacate the building. Had they panicked, hundreds might have been killed. As it was, they took their anger outside, where they indulged in a frenzy of looting and destroying property along Ste. Catherine Street. The ugly riot had a huge impact on the playoff games that followed.

Dick's father was coach of the Montreal Canadiens in 1955. Dick's friend Red Fisher was embarking on a career as a sportswriter, and he just happened to be assigned to cover his first Habs game that fateful March night. Only seconds after he'd taken his seat behind the Red Wing bench, Fisher was struck in the face with a rotten egg. He can laugh about it now, but it wasn't funny at the time.

It wouldn't be the last egg to be tossed that night. Over 16,000 fans were watching the game—all of them in a surly mood. The mood turned to anger and frustration when the Red Wings scored four first-period goals. When Campbell, accompanied by his secretary, arrived almost 15 minutes after the opening faceoff, the fans found a target for their pent-up anger and rage.

When Campbell took his seat, the crowd stood and booed. Then came the missiles. Programs, peanuts, toe rubbers, more eggs. Campbell did not flee. Stoically, he tried to wait out the storm. He even smiled once or twice.

He had been warned not to come. During the past 24 hours he'd received a number of threatening phone calls. One caller had told his secretary, "When I catch up to Campbell, I will kill him!" A woman had shouted a warning, "Don't show up at the Forum or you'll be murdered."

Most of the policemen on duty at the Forum that night appeared to be unwilling to protect Campbell from the howling mob that moved closer to him during the first intermission. Perhaps they were thinking, "The fool should have stayed home. Now he's going to cause us all kinds of trouble."

Overnight, the cerebral Campbell, a former referee, a lawyer, a war crimes prosecutor at Nuremberg, and now NHL president, had become the most detested man in the hockey-mad province of Quebec. On the previous day, Campbell had made the bold and highly controversial decision to suspend Richard, the idol of all of French Canada, not for a game or two, but for the rest of the season *and the entire playoffs*. The move had shocked Montrealers and triggered an outburst of unbelievable animosity toward the solemn-faced Campbell.

Ignored or dismissed was the fact that Richard had been on Campbell's carpet on several occasions. He'd paid more fines for misconduct than any other player in history. The playoffs were about to begin, and for Richard to be barred from them was intolerable. What's more, not only would Richard miss a chance to bring Montreal a Stanley Cup, he would be denied a chance to win the individual scoring race—a prize he had never captured. It meant that teammate Bernard Geoffrion, a poor imitation of the Rocket, would skate off with the Art Ross Trophy.

There weren't enough ugly words in the language—French or English—to describe how Richard supporters felt about Campbell. His cruelty was unforgivable. Surely it was another example of an Anglo punishing a French-Canadian. "If the Rocket's last name was Richardson, he'd have received a mere slap on the wrist," wrote one reporter.

What wasn't reported, until Habs executive Ken Reardon mentioned it to Dick Irvin years later, was that Richard's fate was sealed even before Campbell's ruling. At a meeting in New York on the day before the suspension was announced, NHL owners met and agreed that Richard must be severely disciplined. "The owners decided he must go," Reardon told Irvin, suggesting that while it was an owners' decision, it would be left to Campbell to announce it—then brace himself to take all the heat.

The first period ended at the Forum.

Fisher, staring in disbelief, saw a young man bull his way past an usher and attack the NHL chief. The man lashed out twice with his fists before the ushers intervened. Another wild-eyed fan rushed in and squashed two tomatoes on Campbell's chest.

"Then I saw Jimmy Orlando move in fast," Red recalls. "Orlando was a pro hockey player who'd been with Detroit. A tough guy. He spun Campbell's attacker around and drilled him—right in the chops. There were teeth flying everywhere."

Then the tear gas bomb went off, not far from where Campbell was sitting. A cloud of smoke rose high in the air. Fans bolted from their seats and headed for the exits. Campbell leaped up and fought his way through the crowd to the Forum clinic, where he huddled with fire department officials. A decision was made to clear the building. Campbell made another decision—to award the game to Detroit.

The public address announcer pleaded with the spectators to stay calm and move along quickly to the exits. Fortunately, there was no real panic; otherwise hundreds might have been trampled in the stampede. Campbell, too, might have been trampled or seriously injured if the bomb hadn't served as a distraction.

Outside the Forum, a huge crowd milled about. Many were young thugs who began throwing missiles that scarred the building and shattered windows. Streetcars were damaged, their trolleys pulled from the overhead wires, stalling traffic in all directions. People with bloodied faces were loaded into police cars, which pushed their way through the throng.

The howling mob moved along Ste. Catherine Street, overturning cars. A newsstand was set afire and bricks and bottles were tossed through shop windows. Looters moved inside and snatched up valuable merchandise. Dozens of rioters, many of them teenagers, were arrested and hauled away. Things didn't calm down until after 3 a.m.

Before the Red Wings left the city, manager Jack Adams delivered a parting shot: "You newspapermen have turned Richard into an idol, a man whose suspension can turn fans into shrieking idiots. Richard is no hero. He let his team down, he let hockey down, and he let the public down."

Richard himself seldom discussed the event in later years, except to say, "It was Mr. Campbell who incited the fans. If he had not gone to the game that night…"

Richard lost the scoring crown that spring, by a single point to Boom

Boom Geoffrion. Many fans unfairly blamed Geoffrion for not passing up scoring opportunities in the handful of games that remained so that Richard could be the winner.

"The fans—they were hard on me. They hurt me," Geoffrion would say. "They threatened my wife and kids. That was a terrible summer for me. And it wasn't my fault."

The ugly riot was blamed for the expulsion of the Habs from the 1955 playoffs. With their star player sidelined, with Beliveau battling an illness, and with their emotions still in turmoil, the Habs were eliminated by the Detroit Red Wings in the finals. The Red Wings captured the first two games on home ice, establishing a record for consecutive victories (15), and they won game seven at the Olympia, where they had not been defeated since December 19, 1954.

To their credit, the Habs stayed on the ice to congratulate the new champions and Red Wings' president Marguerite Norris, the first woman officially connected to the NHL to have her name engraved on the Stanley Cup. The previous year the Habs had snubbed the winners and had been criticized in the press for their poor sportsmanship.

Referee Quits After Playoff Fiasco

Throughout the 1950s, Red Storey, a former football star who once scored three touchdowns for the Toronto Argonauts in a Grey Cup game, established himself as one of the most colourful, popular, and highly respected referees in the NHL. But his illustrious career came to a shocking end during the Stanley Cup playoffs in 1959.

On April 4, 1959, the Montreal Canadiens, pitted against the Chicago Blackhawks in game six of a best-of-seven semifinal series at the cavernous Chicago Stadium, held a three-games-to-two lead. Storey's work over the first two periods of a spectacular see-saw game drew nods of approval from Chicago coach Billy Reay and Montreal's bench boss, Toe Blake. Earlier in the series, Reay had pleaded with referee-in-chief Carl Voss to assign the unflappable Storey to referee game six. Before the third period was over, Reay would regret making that request.

It was an emotional match that was tied 3–3 in the third period. At one point, Storey stopped by the boards and turned to see a fan pointing a gun at him. "I'm going to blow your brains out," the man threatened, before two cops moved in and tossed the gun-toter from the rink.

With seven minutes left in the third period, Ed Litzenberger, Chicago's leading scorer, went sprawling after he stepped on Marcel Bonin's stick blade.

No whistle, no penalty to Bonin. The Chicago fans, anticipating a power play, were stunned. They howled in frustration. Moments later, they howled even louder when the Habs scored on Glenn Hall to take a 4–3 lead. The boos rained down on Storey. With two minutes to play, and the score tied 4–4, Bobby Hull, in his second season, was flattened by a hip check thrown by Junior Langlois. It may have been a legal check, but not a soul in the Chicago Stadium thought so. Again, Storey's whistle remained silent.

While the enraged fans screamed at Storey, Montreal's Claude Provost scored the go-ahead goal.

Bottles, cans, coins, programs rained down on the ice—all of the debris aimed at Storey's balding head. Suddenly, a fan vaulted over the boards and ran at Storey, throwing a cupful of beer in his face. Before Storey could react, Montreal's all-star defenceman Doug Harvey skated over and punched the intruder—hard.

"Doug saw I had hauled my fist back and he yelled at me, 'Red, don't hit him. You can't hit him. But I can.' With that, Harvey drilled the guy, not once but twice. Was I glad to see Harvey standing next to me that night.

"From another direction, a second fan skidded across the ice and leaped on my back. I used a move from my pro football days and flipped him high in the air. Almost gleefully, Harvey used his stick this time, lashing out and cutting the fan for about 18 stitches. Thanks to Harvey's lance work, other fans began to have second thoughts about coming out to beat me up. There was a long delay while the ice was cleared. The game continued and Montreal won by a goal—5–4."

In the corridor after the game, Storey grabbed a hockey stick to defend himself from the irate fans and at least one player. The Hawks' fiery Ted Lindsay threatened to decapitate him.

Storey and his two linesmen required a police escort to get back to their hotel long after the game was over. There, in the bar and nursing a couple of beers, Storey heard the bartender shout out, "Keep your eyes open, Red. There was a guy in here a few minutes ago. He had a gun and said he was going to murder you."

Storey didn't relax until he was out of town, bound for Boston and the first game of the final series.

On the following day, he picked up a Boston paper and got the shock of his life. NHL president Clarence Campbell had told an Ottawa reporter that "Storey choked in Chicago. He missed the tripping call on Litzenberger and the penalty that should have gone to Langlois."

Storey demanded an explanation. Campbell tried to explain that his remarks had been "off the record and taken out of context," but Storey had had enough. He resigned on the spot. He refused to speak to Campbell for years, and he called referee-in-chief Voss "the weakest man I've ever met."

Hockey lost a great referee when it lost Red Storey.

Storey was a great storyteller and banquet speaker. He told me once he was accosted by Boston Bruins stalwart Fern Flaman, who was incensed over one of Storey's calls.

"Flaman stood in front of me nose to nose. I expected a tirade, but Flaman said nothing. He just fumed and glared at me. I could feel his hot breath on my face. Finally I said, 'Fernie, why are you standing there like that? What's the matter with you?'

"He snarled, 'Red, I've got the lousiest cold in Boston and I'm standing here until you catch it!' I almost laughed but I caught myself. Then I told him, 'Fernie, that's the same cold I had last week when I was here. I'm glad it was you who caught it.'"

Gadsby Never Got a Sip

One has to feel sorry for Hall of Fame defenceman Bill Gadsby, who played NHL hockey for two decades (1,248 games with Chicago, New York, and Detroit) and never got to sip from the Stanley Cup.

Gadsby shrugs off the disappointment. "I had a long career during the Original Six era," he says. "I was lucky. Fewer than 50 defenceman made it to the NHL in those days."

Gadsby figures he knows a thing or two about good luck. As a 12-year-old in 1939, he survived the sinking of the *Athenia* after a German U-boat torpedoed it. The *Athenia*, bound for Montreal with 1,004 passengers, went down off the northwest coast of Ireland on September 3, 1939, the day of the outbreak of World War II.

The U-boat captain, Fritz-Julius Lemp, disobeyed Hitler's orders not to sink passenger ships. Lemp called the *Athenia* an "armed merchant cruiser," torpedoed her, and fled the scene. At least 112 passengers and crew went down with the ship. Gadsby and his mother spent hours in a lifeboat before being rescued.

A few years later, at the start of his hockey career, Gadsby conquered polio when that disease was a crippling menace. "That was a worrisome time, but again, I was lucky.

"I reached the Stanley Cup finals three times as a Red Wing late in my career," he says. "In 1966, I was convinced I was finally going to be on a Cup winner. We had the Montreal Canadiens on the ropes after we won the first two games at the Montreal Forum. We had the momentum and Roger Crozier, our little goalie, was sensational in those games. He won the Conn Smythe Trophy that season." [Author's note: In 43 playoff seasons, the Conn Smythe Trophy has gone to a member of the losing team in the finals just five times: Crozier in 1966, Glenn Hall in 1968, Reggie Leach in 1976, Ron Hextall in 1987, and Jean-Sebastien Giguere in 2003.]

"Anyway, Montreal stormed back to win the next two games in Detroit. That rattled us a bit. And Crozier got banged up in game four. Then the Habs captured game five back in Montreal by a lopsided score. By then the old Cup seemed to be slipping away from the Wings—and me—again! But I still had my hopes up.

"Fortunately, we got hot in game six at the Olympia and we came to the end of regulation time with the score tied. The overtime period got underway. We needed one goal to force a seventh game. The extra period was only a couple of minutes old when Henri Richard raced in on Crozier, calling for a pass. The puck came to him just as he fell down. Well, both Richard and the puck slid into the net, but the little bugger shoved the puck in with his arm. I saw him do it! Then all the Canadiens poured out on the ice. I turned and stared at the referee, waiting for him to wave off the goal. But he didn't wave it off. I'm telling you he should have. Everybody knows you can't score a goal by pushing the puck in the net. And that's what Richard did.

"For years now I've talked about that illegal goal. But they counted it, and I knew that day it was going to be my last chance to play on a Cup winner.

"And hey, you know who agreed with me on that call? John Ferguson did. And his coach, Toe Blake. Blake was a smart man, though. And quick to react. He was so afraid the goal would be disallowed he sent his players over the boards to start celebrating. He figured with all his players on the ice jumping around and pounding Richard on the back the referee would be distracted. The commotion would prevent him from conferring with the goal judge or the linesmen. It worked, too."

Years later, your correspondent asked Frank Udvari, the referee in the game Gadsby can't forget, about Richard's series-winning goal. He agreed it was a controversial way to end a final series. "Dave Balon fired the pass to Richard, but he took it on the arm or shoulder as he was sliding headfirst toward the goal. Richard went into the net and the puck went in with him. So I called it a goal."

John Ferguson called the ending of that game "as weird and anticlimactic as you could imagine." Fergie chuckled and added, "The goal probably should have been disallowed. Richard slid a good 10 yards down the ice and into the net with the puck. Udvari seemed stunned, mummified. If he'd called it off, we wouldn't have had a gripe.

Ferguson was on the Montreal bench. "When the goal was scored, Toe kept yelling at us, 'Get on the ice! Get on the ice!' " he recalls. "I guess we froze, thinking the goal wouldn't count. It was a smart move by Toe, getting us over the boards. Maybe it caused Udvari to swallow his whistle. And the Red Wings appeared to be in a trance, not beefing very much. It was a peculiar ending to a final series, but we were very happy with the result. I remember Bill Gadsby fuming. He looked about as frustrated and glum as I've ever seen him. He knew it was his last chance. He was ready to retire."

Horton Would Have Won the Smythe Trophy

As each NHL game came to a close on *Hockey Night in Canada*, in the gondola over Maple Leaf Gardens, Bill Hewitt and I would list our choices for the game's three stars. Our votes, along with those of Dave Hodge and Bob Goldham, would be tabulated, and Paul Morris, the Gardens' public-address announcer, would announce the post-game selections.

On February 20, 1974, late in the game between the Buffalo Sabres and the Leafs, there was a commercial break.

"Who do you like for the three stars?" Bill asked me.

"I like Tim Horton, for one," I answered. "For a guy 44 years old, he played a strong game tonight for the Sabres."

"But he didn't play much in the third period," Bill replied. "Maybe one shift."

"I know. He's nursing a very sore jaw. He stopped a Rene Robert slap shot in practice yesterday. But he was splendid for 40 minutes tonight."

At game's end, Horton was named one of the three stars, but he did not appear for the traditional quick skate to acknowledge the honour. He was in too much pain.

I learned later that he met with his family and friends, took some pain killers, then began driving back to Buffalo in his new Ford Pantera sports car, a gift from Buffalo manager Punch Imlach and the Sabres.

He never got to the border.

En route to Buffalo, Horton stopped at the offices of Tim Hortons Inc. in Oakville, where he visited with Ron Joyce, his partner in the fledgling donut business. At around 4:00 a.m., Horton sped away toward Buffalo. In St. Catharines, driving at more than 100 miles per hour, with police cars in pursuit, he lost control of the Pantera and it somersaulted wildly. Without a seat belt to restrain him, Horton was thrown out of the passenger-side door and was killed almost instantly.

Hockey fans everywhere went into mourning when they heard the news the following day.

Horton's NHL career, which spanned more than 20 years, was marked by many triumphs along with that final tragedy.

Perhaps his greatest performance came in the spring of 1962, when the Leafs met the Blackhawks in the Stanley Cup finals. The series went to a seventh game at the mammoth Chicago Stadium. With the scored tied 1–1, Horton burst out of the Leaf zone on a power play. "I threw the puck over to Army [George Armstrong], who went in deep," he recalled. "Army slipped it back to me and I sent it over to Dick Duff, who scored a great goal to win the game."

Horton's assist gave him 16 playoff points—a new NHL record for points by a defenceman.

His regular-season play in 1961–62 had also been superb, and yet, to the chagrin of his fans and family, the First Team All-Star berths were captured by Montreal's Doug Harvey and Jean-Guy Talbot. Second-team positions were awarded to Tim's teammate Carl Brewer and the Blackhawks' Pierre Pilote.

Horton would surely have been named winner of the Conn Smythe Trophy as playoff MVP in 1962 but for the fact the award hadn't been invented yet. It was introduced in 1965.

What's more, Horton's name might well have been associated with the team of the century—1972's Team Canada. It's not generally known that Horton turned down an invitation to play for the team that edged the Soviets on Paul Henderson's famous goal. He did so because of his loathing for the man who organized the series—Alan Eagleson.

I recall Tim Horton as a man of great strength, with fierce loyalty to his team, the backbone of a club that won four Stanley Cups.

Dave Keon says, "Tim was a great teammate, player and friend. He was a leader, a wonderful person."

Bobby Hull, an opponent who was often frustrated by Horton's defensive play, said: "He had tremendous strength and he would use it to keep you in check. He brought honour and dedication to the game."

The late Leaf Billy Harris recalled Tim Horton's devilish sense of humour. "On a train ride one night, we decided to 'initiate' Foster Hewitt. Hindsight says it was a dumb idea, but we went to Hewitt's berth, Timmy slipped his big arms under Hewitt's body and pulled him from the berth. Well, one look at Foster said it all. He was terrified. Tim looked down at him, felt Foster's body twitching and shaking, and said with a grin, 'Well, Foster, I guess we'll save this initiation for another day.' And he returned Foster to the berth."

At training camp one year, Tim was holding out for a better contract and manager Punch Imlach of the Leafs stubbornly refused to give in. Horton, just getting involved in the donut business, sent Imlach a box of the stalest, mouldiest donuts he could find. There was a note inside. "Do you think a man who can produce a superior product like this needs to play hockey for a living?"

Imlach laughed, called Horton in, and they quickly reached an agreement.

It's understandable that Horton would be seeking more money from the Leafs. In 1960–61, when the average salary for the team was about $12,700, Horton was paid much less than Red Kelly, who earned $21,000 (counting bonuses), Bert Olmstead ($19,500), Frank Mahovlich ($18,250), Bob Pulford ($15,500), Allan Stanley ($15,500), and Johnny Bower (who signed for $11,500 but earned bonus money of $4,000). Tightwad Imlach paid team captain George Armstrong a mere $14,000, and Tim Horton (with bonus money) $13,100. Players like Carl Brewer, Bob Baun, and Ron

Stewart received less than that. And rookie of the year Dave Keon was paid a pittance—$8,000.

Horton's final contract with Buffalo was believed to be in the $125,000 range.

By 1999, sales of Tim Hortons had reached $400 million. Prior to that, Tim's widow Lori sold her interest in the business for $1 million.

Carl the Cup Maker

Many years ago, back in the early 1960s, your author had an interesting conversation with a silversmith in Montreal. I was surprised to learn that he had an interest in hockey and even more surprised when he told me he had created an exact duplicate of the Stanley Cup. His name was Carl Petersen.

Brian: Mr. Petersen, tell us about your association with the Stanley Cup and your role in its preservation.

Petersen: First, let me say how proud I am to be able to play a role in the history of this fine trophy. Many years ago, I began working on the Cup—you know, two or three times each season. I would add new names and bands when needed and I would fix it up. Now it is in a first-class condition. Sometimes I wish the players would take better care of it when they win it. But they are young and always so full of joy and enthusiasm. I'm afraid sometimes they get a little careless with it. But I suppose that is understandable.

Brian: As I understand it, the original bowl that Lord Stanley donated to hockey in 1893 is not the bowl we see on the Stanley Cup now.

Petersen (*smiling*): No, you see, some years ago I spoke to Mr. Clarence Campbell, the league president, and I said, "Mr. Campbell, if you lose that bowl on top, the original bowl, if somebody knocks it off and breaks it, it can't be replaced. I can't make another one. That is the most precious piece of the whole trophy."

Mr. Campbell said, "Mr. Petersen, do you think you can make an exact duplicate in your shop, one that we can exchange with the original Cup and nobody will even know?"

I said, "Sure I can, Mr. Campbell. You will be amazed. It will be exactly like the bowl that's been on top for decades."

So he authorized me to go ahead and do it. I began making him another Stanley Cup exactly like the first one. The original bowl, I kept in my shop on and off for three years. And nobody ever asked me, "Carl, why is the Stanley Cup in your shop and not in the league office or the Hall of Fame?" So I didn't have to invent any stories. I made Mr. Campbell a beautiful new bowl. Even the scratch marks that I noticed on the original went on the new one. You can't tell the difference. The old one now is in the Hockey Hall of Fame, where it's kept in a bank vault. But you can go and see it. Now, if somebody steals the new one someone like myself can easily make another one.

Now we move forward to 1994 and witness the angry reaction of Carl Petersen's son Ole when he learned about a Cup prank orchestrated by New York Ranger forward Ed Olczyk.

Olczyk took the Stanley Cup to Belmont Park a few days after the Rangers won it. There he was photographed, apparently treating 1994 Kentucky Derby winner Go For Gin to a snack of oats from the bowl of the trophy. Some people thought it was in poor taste—pardon the pun. The photo enraged 67-year-old Ole Petersen, , whose late father had a decades-old association with the trophy.

When Ole saw Go For Gin's snout in the bowl of the Cup, he was stunned. "I can't believe the Stanley Cup is being treated with such a lack of respect," he said indignantly. "My father redesigned the Cup in 1962, making a perfect replica of the original bowl. He must be spinning in his grave. This is mind-boggling. The reputation of the Cup has certainly been tarnished.

Imagine a horse eating out of it. What if the Mona Lisa was taken from the Louvre, hung in a mall, and kids were allowed to throw spitballs at it? What that Ranger player did is unpardonable."

Olczyk later explained that the Kentucky Derby winner didn't actually dine from the Stanley Cup. "It just looked that way," he said. "It was a publicity shot. There was no food in the Cup, no water. I can't believe that the photo upset so many people. Especially after all the other bizarre things that have happened to the Cup."

If Ole Petersen had been told that the Cup had survived some rather disgusting treatment by certain players over the years, he would have been totally disgusted and infuriated. Surely he would have demanded that anyone showing such lack of respect for such a venerated trophy should be imprisoned for life.

The Cup Thief

There he was in the spring of 1962, sitting in a bar in Chicago, wearing his favourite jacket with the Montreal Canadiens logo on the front and crossed Canadian and American flags on the sleeve. It was the kind of jacket we all wore back then. They were popular in the early '60s.

His name was Ken Kilander, a native Montrealer. He was a musician, a piano player who held a summer job as a lifeguard in Atlantic City. He was 25 years old, husky and ruddy-faced, and a hockey fan like no other. He adored the Canadiens, so attached to the team that he often followed them on road trips.

He paid for his travel and game tickets by playing piano in bars in the six NHL cities, always close to the arenas. Players and fans noticed him hanging around, got to know him. They even came to the bars to hear him play.

His favourite hockey player was Boom Boom Geoffrion. "But I liked the guys from other teams, too," he stated. "I liked Red Kelly and Eddie Shack. They always said hello and asked me how I was, what I'd been doing."

None of the players, or any of his acquaintances, would expect this wandering musician to make headlines that very night—by stealing the Stanley Cup, hockey's most coveted trophy.

But that's exactly what Kilander did.

In the bar that day, Kilander chatted with some Montreal reporters, in town to cover the semifinal series between the Hawks and the Habs.

"I'm here to watch my Canadiens win a Stanley Cup game," Kilander told them. "I've just come from the Chicago Stadium. The Cup is on display in the lobby there. It's inside a glass showcase."

"But the Canadiens trail in the series three games to two," one of the reporters told him. "If your Habs lose tonight, they're finished."

"It looks like curtains for Montreal," said another scribe. "Henri Richard is out with a broken arm and coach Toe Blake blew his stack in the last game and assaulted a referee."

"Still, Montreal should have the Cup," Kilander insisted. "Not Chicago. My Canadiens finished in first place, 23 points ahead of the Blackhawks."

The reporters chuckled. "I predict the Cup will stay right here in Chicago," one of them said. "Glenn Hall and Bobby Hull will see to that."

"No, no, it's going back to Montreal," was Kilander's retort. Then he threw out a bold challenge. "What would you say if I told you I can get the Stanley Cup and bring it back to the hotel—and give it to the Canadiens?"

The reporters laughed out loud. "I'd say you're crazy," one of them told him. "But if you do steal the Cup, you'll get your name in a lot of papers. And your photo, too."

"Then I'll do it," Kilander vowed.

He went to the game that night. In the lobby of the Stadium, he examined the showcase housing the Stanley Cup.

"Hmm," he murmured. "That lock is not very strong. Barely adequate."

He took his seat and watched the first two periods of the game. He was in agony as his beloved Habs were badly outplayed. At the midway mark of the third period, the situation was hopeless. The Blackhawks were leading 4–1.

Fuming, Kilander left his seat and wandered back into the arena lobby. There was nobody around. He stood in front of the showcase and pushed on the glass. The lock gave way. He removed the Stanley Cup and hoisted it onto his shoulder.

Stealthily, he strode toward an exit leading to the street outside. Just then, an usher arrived on the scene.

"Hey! Where are you going with the Cup?" he demanded. "Put it back!"

"I will not," Kilander stated, pushing on the door. "I'm taking it back to Montreal. That's where it belongs."

The usher, 21-year-old Michael Frain, began to holler. "Someone's stealing the Stanley Cup. Help! Help! Someone stop him!"

Stadium police heard the shouts and came running. They found Kilander wrestling the Cup through the half-open door. Kilander was quickly apprehended, arrested, and taken to jail.

"I knew he was up to no good," young Frain said, proud that he was able to prevent the theft. "The goofball was wearing a jacket with a Montreal crest on the front."

Someone arrived from the Hawks' front office and took the Cup away. It was placed in a crate and stored safely in the Blackhawks' dressing room.

Kilander appeared in a Chicago court on the following morning and faced an angry judge.

"You'd better get back to Montreal, young man," he scolded, "or I'll put you behind bars. And you'd better give up any idea of taking the Cup with you."

"Yes, sir, Your Honour."

His media pals were right about one thing: Kilander got a lot of press attention after his theft of the Cup. His photo was in all the papers, even as far away as New York.

"When I heard about his caper, I immediately barred him from all games at Madison Square Garden," said Muzz Patrick, general manager of the Rangers. "After all, the Stanley Cup is a sacred thing. Nobody should be stealing it."

When asked if he had any advice for the Montrealer, Patrick said, "Yes, I do. He should stick to piano playing. I've heard him. He's a damn fine player."

Billy Harris's Stanley Cup Memories

The late Billy Harris, a popular member of the Toronto Maple Leafs from 1957 to 1965, enjoyed reminiscing about the sixties and the three Cup-winning teams he played on. Prior to his death at age 65 in September, 2001, he talked to me candidly about the players—and his coach—from that era:

Brian: Bill, tell me about Bert Olmstead and his importance to the Leafs.

Billy: I've often said if we didn't get Bert Olmstead from the Canadiens in '58, I don't think that we would have won our first Stanley Cup in '62. We had so much direction from Bert, especially the younger players. We learned what pride was all about and how important it was to win a Stanley Cup when you have an opportunity. Unfortunately for Bert, one day Conn Smythe made a comment to a Toronto writer that he thought Bert Olmstead had the qualities to be the next Maple Leaf coach. We won the Stanley Cup in April of 1962 and Punch Imlach very quickly dropped Bert's name from our protected list. I think, in a pre-arranged deal, the New York Rangers drafted Bert, knowing Bert wasn't interested in moving to another city. Bert went to training camp that year and never put the uniform on and never negotiated another contract, and retired from hockey.

Brian: Was Imlach that insecure?

Billy: I think that Punch, even when he won the Stanley Cup, felt very insecure and couldn't get rid of Olmstead quickly enough, because as I said, he was afraid Bert might become the next Maple Leaf coach.

Brian: Well, Punch was a complex guy and treated so many people in a bizarre manner. I think of Brewer and Mahovlich and, well, any number of them. Did he rule by fear?

Billy: You mentioned the two in particular—Mahovlich and Brewer. I think that Punch got about maybe 40 or 50 percent of the potential out of those two athletes. Punch treated the team as a regiment, and I think individuals like Mahovlich and Brewer, if they'd had a coach that could communicate one on one, I think it would have made a big difference in getting the full value out of Mahovlich and Brewer. In this day and age, we have learned you can't treat 20 athletes in the same manner. It's a one-on-one situation. If the coach or general manager is good at communicating one on one, he's going to get a much better total effort out of his team.

For example, Ronnie Stewart—you can yell and scream at him, making him do stops and starts for an hour and a half, and maybe he'll play better the next game. But you can't treat sensitive people like Mahovlich and Brewer that way and expect them to give you 100 percent. Punch didn't even take the trouble to learn how to pronounce Mahovlich. It always came out "Maholovich." That often puzzled me.

Brian: He must have been an intimidating presence in the Leaf dressing room.

Billy: I think, especially after we had won a Stanley Cup or two in Toronto, Imlach's position became that much stronger and I think that people like Shack and Mahovlich were intimidated by him. They felt they had to back Punch—or else. In those days, Brian, if Punch didn't like the way you practised or didn't like the way you reacted to things he said, you could be on your way down to Rochester. So the guy running the show intimidated the guys that were insecure. Frank and Punch did not have a good relationship, from my view. I believe that Frank probably played the best hockey of his career in his last three years in the NHL, when he was with Montreal, where I think he was totally relaxed. Sam Pollock made him feel comfortable in Montreal. He was there for three years and was on two Stanley Cup teams. So, if there had been an atmosphere in Toronto where there had been a better relationship between Imlach and Mahovlich, Frank might have scored 60 or 70 goals for the Leafs.

Brian: Punch knew how to wield his power.

Billy: Well, I played seven years for Punch Imlach and got to know him quite well. I can remember talking to a good friend of mine, Johnny Robertson, who wrote for the *Toronto Star*. Punch called him in one day, and there was a file of all the Leaf stories Johnny had written. Punch told him, "You have no right to say this. You have no right to say that. Why did you do this? Why did you do that?" And so on. Punch kept a diary on people. Maybe he wouldn't hear your comments live, but someone—his wife, Dodo, maybe—would tell him what you had said and he kept a file on those types of things. If a person is secure in their job, they don't do that. But Punch, if you said something that he didn't like, and you were a member of the media, you'd hear from him. He had that kind of clout, especially with success. He had a lot of power.

Brian: There were so many interesting players on those clubs that you played with. There was Shack and Bower, Horton and Red Kelly. I marvel that Kelly could play hockey and serve as a member of Parliament. That was really an amazing situation that he was in.

Billy: Well, it was quite a mixture of personalities. It was incredible that Red was able to commute to Ottawa, do his job there as a member of Parliament, and be at practice the next day. During games, I remember sitting in the dressing room not far from where Kelly and Timmy Horton sat. They used to sleep between periods. Johnny Bower used to give them a signal by whacking his stick on the dressing room floor when Imlach came around the corner. I guess that was when Kelly caught up with his rest. Red was dedicated. I can't think of any other athlete who could have combined being a member of Parliament and being a professional athlete at the same time.

We had humorous people like Eddie Shack and George Armstrong. We had serious people like Red Kelly and Allan Stanley. We had the right chemistry. It was a really interesting group. And from that mix, we became Stanley Cup champions.

Brian: And Bower? Johnny was a huge factor in your success.

Billy: It was amazing that he was able to come up from Cleveland at age 33 or whatever he was. And he stayed around long enough to win the Stanley Cup four times and become a Hall of Famer. Young kids today look at you kind of funny when you tell them a story like that. I can think of a few goaltenders that I played against that had more ability than Johnny Bower. But if you ask me to pick a guy that you'd like to have there in the seventh game of a Stanley Cup final, I'd pick Johnny Bower. Johnny is a winner! Johnny is great! And one thing that made him great, Brian, is that I can never, ever remember him having a goal scored on him where he pointed a finger at a defenceman or blamed somebody else. Every goal that was scored on Johnny Bower, he blamed himself. I think that has a tremendous impact on how your teammates play in front of you.

I remember Harry Lumley, who was a goalie for the Leafs, and Harry was notorious for glaring and pointing a finger at the guy that he thought was responsible for a goal that was scored.

Brian: What about Sawchuk?

Billy: What a contrast between the two goaltenders! Johnny Bower loved to practise; Terry Sawchuk hated to practise. Bower would be the first guy on the ice at practice, the last guy off. Sawchuk would be the last guy on and first off. He hated guys shooting at him in practice. But when you think of the great ones, Sawchuk has a record that nobody will ever beat—103 shutouts. When you think of Sawchuk, you think of Jacques Plante and you think of Bower. Three of the greatest!

Brian: Who else made you proud to have as a teammate?

Billy: The closest friend I had in hockey was Timmy Horton. For 10 years, every Sunday on the road trips, Tim and I went to church together. Now, Catholics always go to church on Sunday. But Tim and I were both Protestants. In every city in the NHL, we'd find a church and go there. In later years, Larry Hillman used to join us, and then Ronnie Ellis. From walking to church and back, I got to know Tim probably as well as any teammate. Unfortunately, at a very young age, he was killed in a car accident. You couldn't replace a Tim Horton. In a very quiet way, he was so dependable, so reliable, his leadership, his work ethic, all of those things. He was probably the closest friend I had as a player and a guy who was extremely valuable to the Leafs and helped them to four Stanley Cups.

Imlach had a unique relationship with Tim. Timmy had a lot of respect for Punch and it was one of those rare cases where a guy like Punch had a lot of respect for, and got along well with, Tim Horton.

Brian: What about Imlach coming back for a second time (in the late 1970s)? He couldn't operate then the way he used to.

Billy: Some people—managers and coaches especially—who were around during the transition when the league expanded from six teams to 12 teams had to adjust quickly or be gone. The game was changing. The challenge of the WHA in the early '70s, which gave players options; negotiating with agents instead of the players themselves. Imlach was one of those hockey men who couldn't make the adjustments. He could handle things when he was kind of a dictator and when there were only six teams; but with expansion and those other things I mentioned, Punch was not able to make the adjustment, and I think that had a lot to do with his problems. That—and a heart attack—ended his career. But he brought Toronto four Stanley Cups. That can never be forgotten.

Baun's Broken-Leg Goal

The Toronto Maple Leafs captured four Stanley Cups in the 1960s and haven't been able to wrap their arms around it since. One of the most talked-about triumphs was the 1964 victory, highlighted by defenceman Bobby Baun's famous broken leg goal.

It happened in game six of the finals, in Detroit on April 23. The Red Wings were ahead in their series against the Leafs, three games to two. One more triumph would bring them the Cup. In the third period, Gordie Howe drilled a shot off Baun's right leg, just above the ankle. Gamely, Baun played on and moments later went up against Howe on a faceoff in the Leaf zone.

"You remember how Howe used to blink a lot? Well, I used to drive him crazy by blinking at him, mocking him. It was my job to distract him, to take him out. Back then, defencemen used to take the faceoffs in their own end, and I won the draw from Howe. I spun around, and that's when I heard a noise like a cannon going off. It was the bone in my leg cracking. I knew it right away. I fell to the ice in front of Bower, my leg feeling like cream cheese above my skate. Before I knew it, I was being carted off on a stretcher. I knew then the bone in my leg was either cracked or broken.

"In the medical room, I asked the team doctor to tape my leg and freeze it. No way did I want them taking x-rays. I really wanted to get back out there. The freezing seemed to work and I hobbled back to the bench and jumped over the boards before Punch Imlach could stop me, just before the period ended. After 60 minutes the score was tied and the game went to overtime.

"During my first shift in overtime—I hadn't been out there more than 20 seconds—the puck came rolling around the boards toward me and I moved to keep it in the Detroit zone. I had time to take a shot so I whacked at it. A ballplayer would describe my shot as a 'knuckleball.' I could see it all the way in. It bounced off Bill Gadsby's stick and somehow found its way past Terry Sawchuk into the Detroit net. It wasn't a classic, but it was my biggest goal ever. Came at 1:43 of overtime."

Gadsby almost wept in frustration. "I didn't see the damn puck until it was too late," he muttered afterward. "Baun's shot ticked my stick and deflected past Sawchuk."

"Two nights later," Baun recalled, "we won the Stanley Cup on home ice by a 4–0 score. I had my leg iced before that game and took shots of Novocaine every 10 minutes. Only after the Cup was won did I go for x-rays, and they found a broken bone just above the ankle. I was in a cast for the next six weeks. Was it worth it? Sure it was. That's how much winning the Stanley Cup meant to me. Most hockey players would tell you they'd do the very same thing."

Gadsby always doubted Baun's story and insisted he was no playoff hero.

"It all bull——," says Gadsby. "His leg wasn't broken. He may have had a hairline fracture, but the media played it up big. I remember skating up to Baun before game seven. I said, 'Who do you think you're kidding?' He just kind of shrugged."

Detroit's Sid Abel agreed. "His so-called injury was just a Leaf gimmick to delay the game," he insists. "And it worked because we cooled off when Baun went down. I was suspicious when he came back so soon. And where did the stretcher come from so fast? Come on. Turns out the Leafs brought their own stretcher. Teams don't do that unless..."

The late Dick Beddoes, an uncommonly clever wordsmith, once challenged

Baun. "You've dined out on the broken leg story for over 25 years," he said accusingly. "It wasn't the big bone in your leg that snapped. It was only the fibula."

"Go take a shit in your hat, Baddies," Baun said amiably.

Gordie Howe had little to say about Baun's winning goal, but years later he became a Baun fan.

Late in his career, Baun wound up in Detroit, playing alongside "Blinky" Howe. Arriving via a trade from the Oakland Seals, Baun took Howe aside one day and said, "Listen to me, you old fart. The Red Wings are screwing you. Do you know I'm making twice as much money as you are?"

"That can't be," said Howe. "The Wings assured me I'm at the top of their payroll."

"Not true," said Baun. "You go in tomorrow and demand a hundred grand a year. I figure you're down for $45,000 and I'm earning double that."

Howe steamed into the Red Wings' front office the next morning and team owner Bruce Norris met his demands—just like that. Norris always believed it was Howe's wife, Colleen, who was behind Gordie's angry demand for a major salary boost. It wasn't. It was Bobby Baun.

Sawchuk's Greatest Game

When a big-league goaltender has played for 21 seasons, performed in 971 games (winning 447), and captured four Stanley Cups, it's almost impossible to pick one game that stands out as his best.

But one I saw and helped broadcast is my choice when people ask, "What's the best game you ever saw Terry Sawchuk play?"

It was the final game of the 1966–67 season, a 3–1 triumph for the Toronto Maple Leafs over the Montreal Canadiens at Maple Leaf Gardens. Toronto fans who witnessed the Leafs topple the Habs four games to two in the final series expected to see Stanley's mug return from time to time in coming seasons. They've been looking—and hoping—but they haven't seen the old chalice since.

Some may find it hard to recall that it was goaltender Terry Sawchuk who was largely responsible for ending the series in game six and who admitted afterward, "This was the greatest thrill of my life."

Nursing a bruised cheekbone, where a shot had dented his mask, he added quietly, "I've enjoyed a lot of wonderful moments in hockey and played on other Stanley Cup teams, but there's been nothing to equal this."

The game's first star, Sawchuk had treated Leaf fans to a classic display of netminding. Among the many shots he faced were 13 key saves—five of them in the first period, when it looked as though the Habs would overwhelm the Leafs and force a seventh game back in Montreal.

"I was going to retire before the season," Sawchuk told reporters. "Remember, I had a back operation and I felt miserable. I almost walked out of training camp. But Punch Imlach talked me into staying. Then I had a physical collapse in mid-season while in the shower in Montreal. Right now, I'm too tired to dance around and celebrate like the younger guys. Guess I'll go call my wife. We have six kids and another on the way. Maybe this is it for me. It's nice to bow out a winner."

Sawchuk came off a bad outing in game four, when he was maligned and taunted by the Gardens' crowd for his shoddy play. Sawchuk gave up half a dozen goals in a 6–2 pounding by the Habs. One irate Leaf fan sent him a telegram: "How much did you get to throw the game?"

Sawchuk vowed to make the fan eat his words.

He was called on in game six after Johnny Bower, his goaltending partner (a winner in game five), pulled a hamstring in the morning skate and could not perform.

Rumours circulated that Sawchuk was in no condition to play, that he'd been drinking heavily the day before the game, that he had already made the assumption that Bower would be Punch Imlach's choice to finish the series.

Perhaps he'd played with a hangover. Who will ever know?

"What a game he played tonight," praised Punch Imlach, emerging from the showers where his players had tossed him, water dripping from his clothes. "If he'd been injured, Johnny Bower couldn't have played, although I had him dressed and on the bench. Bower's groin injury wouldn't have allowed it. So I had Gary Smith, my third goalie, dressed and ready to go, sitting in the dressing room. Nobody knew about Smith. But Sawchuk never looked better than he did tonight."

Imlach claimed the Leafs, who'd finished third in the standings, deserved to be called a great Stanley Cup team.

"We beat two powerful clubs to get here, didn't we?" he asked. "So we have to be called great. Chicago finished 19 points ahead of us in the standings and

Montreal was only two points back of the Hawks. Nobody gave us a chance. So this was the sweetest of my four Stanley Cup wins. A lot of wise guys said we were too old, too beat up, that we couldn't beat Chicago in the semis or Montreal in the finals. Well, we shoved it right down their throats. Bower and Sawchuk, both older than dirt, were tremendous. And Sawchuk sure as hell ruined Montreal's plans to display the Stanley Cup at Expo 67."

Habs' goalie Rogie Vachon made a surprise exit in the third period of the final game. He was replaced by 38-year-old Gump Worsley, who hadn't played since March 12, when he was struck on the head by an egg thrown by an imbecilic Ranger fan. Worsley responded with 10 fine saves.

A postscript: Sawchuk did not retire after the Leafs won the Cup. He played 36 games with Los Angeles the following season. And 13 games with Detroit in 1968–69. He finished his career with the Rangers, where he played eight games in 1969–70 at age 40. In New York, he recorded his 103rd career shutout—an NHL record that has stood for nearly four decades.

Following the 1969–70 season, Sawchuk and Ranger teammate Ron Stewart became involved in an unfortunate alcohol-induced shoving match late one night. Sawchuk fell and injured himself badly, suffering a lacerated liver. Later, blood clots had to be removed, but one stopped his heart on May 31, 1970. Stewart was cleared of any responsibility for the incident.

Sawchuk was elected posthumously to the Hockey Hall of Fame in 1971 and was awarded the Lester Patrick Trophy for his contributions to hockey in the United States. He is buried in Mount Hope Cemetery near Pontiac, Michigan.

Final Goal of the Original Six Era

When the Montreal Canadiens clashed with the underdog Toronto Maple Leafs in the Stanley Cup finals of 1967, it marked the end of the Original Six era in the NHL. By the time the following season rolled around, six new clubs—expansion teams in Minnesota, Philadelphia, St. Louis, Los Angeles, Oakland, and Pittsburgh—would be in the league. Everything was about to change dramatically. The expansion draft would send players from the original six teams scurrying in all directions.

High in the gondola at Maple Leaf Gardens, while the Habs and Leafs warmed up prior to game six, my broadcast partner, Bill Hewitt, said to me, "I wonder if we'll see the final goal of the Original Six scored tonight."

"We will if the Leafs win," I countered. "If they don't, Montrealers will get to see it—in game seven."

It was May 2, 1967, and the final goal was scored that night—very late in the game. It entered a net vacated moments earlier by goalie Gump Worsley as the Canadiens tried desperately to score the tying goal and prolong the series. How appropriate that Bill's father, Foster Hewitt, the legendary broadcaster, was on hand to describe it:

The crowd can hardly contain themselves during this dramatic struggle. It has been a terrific game all the way. Now someone has thrown what appears to be an egg on the ice and the scrapers are coming out. It is rather unusual for any object to be thrown on Gardens ice, but the delay may be a great help to both clubs because all players seem to be almost exhausted.

Beliveau has been the Montreal leader while Davey Keon for the Leafs has been here, there and everywhere. Both [Montreal goalie Gump] Worsley and [Toronto goalie Terry] Sawchuk have been outstanding, the latter truly sensational.

There are only 55 seconds of regulation time remaining. Toronto leads two goals to one. The hometown crowd is anticipating a Stanley Cup victory in this sixth game, while Montreal Canadiens are using every strategy to get the tying goal and push the game into overtime.

With less than a minute remaining, Leafs are called for icing and the referee calls for a faceoff to the left of Sawchuk. There's a delay in play and Montreal goalkeeper Gump Worsley doesn't know whether or not coach Toe Blake wants him to come out of the net. Now Blake has decided to remove Worsley. He's going to the bench. With 55 seconds to play, Montreal will use six attackers and their goal is empty. Canadiens intend to shoot the works. Beliveau is coming on the ice; so are Roberts, Cournoyer, Ferguson, Henri Richard and Laperriere. It's all or nothing for them now.

Leafs, too, are making changes. Imlach is making his stand with an all-veteran lineup of Stanley, Horton, Kelly, Pulford and Armstrong. Sawchuk, of course, is in goal. Beliveau will face off for Montreal and Stanley for Toronto.

Referee John Ashley is growing impatient. Ferguson skates over to talk to Beliveau. Stanley is hesitating, now he comes into position. This faceoff is vital. They're all set. The puck is dropped. Stanley gets possession; he snaps the puck to Kelly and Kelly kicks it up to Pulford. Pulford passes to Armstrong, who is driving hard. Army shoots toward the empty net. He's on target. *It's in! He scores!* Armstrong has scored the insurance goal. It's now Leafs three, Canadiens one. Toe Blake's strategy has backfired, and that shot just about decided possession of the Stanley Cup. Canadiens had to gamble everything and lost. Time of the goal was 19:23—only 47 seconds left in the game.

Worsley has returned to the Montreal net and play has resumed. Now there are seven seconds left, six, five, four, three, two, one. THE GAME IS OVER! Leafs have won the Stanley Cup. The crowd is going wild. There's no use trying to talk against that uproar. By their well-earned victory, the Toronto Maple Leafs are Stanley Cup champions for 1966–67, their fourth triumph in six years. A truly great record.

If Leaf fans in 1967 were to be told a new century would arrive before another Stanley Cup was held high by Toronto players, they wouldn't have believed it.

Foster Hewitt would never call another Stanley Cup final game. His swan song came in 1972, when he brought millions of Canadians the play-by-play of the memorable Canada–Soviet series, which culminated in Paul Henderson's winning goal in the final seconds of game eight.

Defenceman Larry Hillman was a member of the '67 Leafs. A dozen years earlier, Hillman became one of the youngest players to see his name engraved on the Stanley Cup. In his rookie season, 1954–55, the 18-year-old defenceman became a member of Detroit's Stanley Cup–winning team. At the time, he never dreamed his career would become such a nomadic one, taking him to eight NHL cities and two more franchises in the WHA. Nor could he have imagined his name would be engraved on the Stanley Cup six times—with Detroit in '55, with Toronto in '62, '63, '64, and '67, and again with Montreal in '69.

How was the '67 Stanley Cup victory party, you might ask? I remember it took place at Stafford Smythe's home and I remember crashing it.

It would have been thoughtful if Leaf management had invited us to the celebration—the guys who'd broadcast their games all season. But it never occurred to them. So three of us sat around after the final game until someone said, "Let's crash the party. We'll go to Staff Smythe's house."

That's what we did. And we walked right in. We sipped Champagne from the Stanley Cup. We took some photos. We saw Eddie Shack dancing his feet off, his face drenched in sweat, bubbles of it dropping off his nose. Heads craned when Gary Smith, the third-string goalie strolled in, a Pamela Anderson lookalike on his arm, cleavage down to her navel. Men gaped, women snickered. It was crowded, it was loud, and it was fun.

After an hour or two, we went home.

As we left, I think we all knew it might be many years before the Leafs would celebrate another Stanley Cup victory. But over 40 of them? And still counting?

IV. Expansion Brings
New Champs

Boston Fans Enraged After Quinn Kayoes Orr

No city in North America will open its heart to an Irishman faster than Boston. Unless his name is Pat Quinn and he plays for the hated Toronto Maple Leafs.

On April 2, 1969, Pat Quinn was a hardrock defenceman for the Leafs who found himself in a playoff series against Bobby Orr, Gerry Cheevers, Phil Esposito, and the powerful Bruins. Esposito had finished the regular season atop the scoring race with an all-time high of 126 points. In game one at the Boston Garden, with one devastating check, Quinn became the most despised man in New England. Why? Because he hit Bobby Orr so hard with a body check that Boston fans feared Orr had suffered a broken neck.

I was in the broadcast booth alongside Bill Hewitt when Quinn nailed the Bruin superstar moving out of the Boston zone—with his head down. Until that point, we hadn't seen anything in the Leafs' performance that would cause us to raise our voices. The Leafs were being pummelled by the Bruins (final score was 10–0). Then we saw Quinn rumble into the Boston zone, determined to stop the league's best defenceman in his tracks. He drilled Bobby Orr, who was coming up fast, cradling the puck. Quinn's shoulder check sent Boston's beloved blueliner crashing to the ice, where he lay unconscious. Later his injury would be diagnosed as whiplash and a concussion. Orr had never been hit so hard in his life.

As they were carrying Orr away, the crowd turned on Quinn, who was sitting calmly in the penalty box. A furious throng surrounded the box and pounded on the glass with their fists. Quinn ignored them, even when they attempted to spit on him and hit him with programs and other debris. A metal change holder (like the ones bus drivers carry) flew into the box and struck Quinn. There was more pounding on the glass and, had it been bashed loose, as tough as he was, Quinn would have been piled on, punched, and kicked. There was a lynch-mob mentality surrounding the penalty box. While the threat to Quinn's safety was ongoing, a policeman in the box took a few moments to lecture Quinn on his aggressive behaviour.

Then, for some reason, the policeman grabbed Quinn, possibly to protect him from flying debris, but Quinn misunderstood and pulled away, breaking a pane of glass with his stick. A second policeman moved in and was cut by the flying Plexiglas. For a moment, it looked as though the blood-thirsty fans would succeed in getting to Quinn and beating him to a pulp. But more of Boston's finest arrived and escorted Quinn to the safety of the Leaf dressing room.

There was no need for Quinn to go back on the ice and play in the third period. The game was hopelessly lost. But Quinn wasn't about to show the Boston crowd he'd knuckled under. Back he came to soldier on, showing the Boston fans he would not be cowed. They peppered him with insults and a barrage of missiles and programs, but he survived to play another day.

Quinn has a vivid memory of that fateful hit. "I saw Bobby coming with his head down and yes, I took a run at him. Maybe he didn't see me; maybe there was no room for him to avoid me. I caught him with my right shoulder and I followed through. I was concerned when his head struck the ice. There was a deathly hush in the Boston Garden when he lay there, not moving a muscle. But it turned to bedlam as soon as they got him off the ice."

"It took some time before Pat and I were able to put that incident behind us," Orr said. "I can't believe it's been almost four decades since Pat kayoed me that day. I may not have liked him very much back then. But over the years he became one of my favourite people in hockey."

As the colour commentator that night on *Hockey Night in Canada*, I recall saying to Bill Hewitt, "Bill, to me that looked like a legitimate check by Quinn—a shoulder check. I'm surprised Orr had his head down and didn't see him coming. I'm even a bit surprised there's going to be a penalty on the play."

I remember that game—and that series—for another reason. It almost ended my career with *Hockey Night in Canada*.

During the game, Leaf coach Punch Imlach ordered scrappy forward Forbes Kennedy to "get out there and start something." Kennedy leaped over the boards and moments later ignited a brawl. In the midst of it, he punched linesman George Ashley in the face, knocking him backwards to the ice.

"Oh, oh," I said to Hewitt. "Kennedy's in trouble now. He'll be fined or suspended, maybe both."

I learned later that Clarence Campbell was furious with me for making those comments. He told my producer, Ralph Mellanby, "How dare McFarlane tell me how to do my job?" And Imlach was irate, saying, "McFarlane got our guy suspended."

Kennedy set a playoff record for penalties that night, collecting four minors, two majors, one 10-minute misconduct, and one game misconduct.

The following day, no doubt heeding my advice, NHL president Clarence Campbell fined Kennedy a thousand dollars and suspended him for four games. He never played another game in the NHL.

Prior to game four at Maple Leaf Gardens, King Clancy, Imlach's assistant, took me aside. "Punch wants to see you. He's pissed off because of what you said about Kennedy being fined and suspended. Punch says Kennedy never touched that guy [Ashley]. He says it's all your fault Kennedy got suspended."

I never did get to talk to Punch, who told several others, "That effin' McFarlane has to go." Later that night, after another loss to the Bruins, to my surprise—and, yes, relief— Imlach was fired.

For years, I worried that I might have erred in describing Kennedy's blow that felled George Ashley. So I asked him once, at a celebrity golf tournament in the Maritimes. "Forbsie, did you really nail Ashley that night in Boston?"

He laughed. "Oh, Brian, I smacked him a good one. And down he went."

"Thanks, Forbes. That's all I wanted to know."

Espo Says Bruins the Best

If you were around to listen to Phil Esposito in the early '70s, he'd tell you, "We are the best. The Boston Bruins are the best team in the world."

And he was right. Boston had a wonderful blend of savvy players, starting with a great money goaltender in Gerry Cheevers. And Bobby Orr patrolling the blue line. Orr could have played defence all alone and rival teams would have had trouble scoring. And when he took off with the puck, opposing goalies gulped and crossed their fingers and hoped he wouldn't make them look like dorks.

Up front, there was Espo and his linemates, Wayne Cashman and Ken Hodge. Then came Johnny Bucyk, Fred Stanfield, and Johnny "Pie" Mckenzie. After that, it was Derek Sanderson, Eddie Westfall, and Wayne Carleton. And coach Milt Schmidt had capable spares in Garnet "Ace" Bailey (who would perish years later aboard a hijacked plane that crashed into the World Trade Center on 9/11), versatile Don Marcotte, and sturdy Jim Lorentz.

It was the season Bobby Orr won the Art Ross Trophy as scoring champ with 120 points, 21 more than Esposito, the runner-up. The Bruins tied Chicago for first place overall with 99 points and met the New York Rangers in the opening round of the playoffs.

The teams detested each other. "We knew if we ousted the Rangers, we would win the Cup," Esposito said. "No other club could compete with us."

Again, Phil was right. The Bruins and the Rangers were tied at two wins apiece when the Bruins surged in the next two, winning both and advancing against the Chicago Blackhawks.

"We were really good against the Hawks," Esposito recalls. "Really good. If my brother Tony hadn't been sensational in goal [for Chicago], we would have killed them."

The Bruins swept Chicago aside and then faced the fledgling St. Louis Blues in the final series for the Cup. It was no contest. The Bruins, looking for another sweep, won three straight against Scotty Bowman's Blues and were only threatened in game four. The Blues led 3–2 at the Boston Garden when Esposito snapped a loose puck past Glenn Hall and tied the score. "That's it," he told his mates. "We've got them now. We're not going back to St. Louis."

Still, the game was tied after three periods and overtime would decide it.

Derek Sanderson, who predicted during the intermission that he'd score the winner, started the overtime facing Red Berenson, the Blues' scoring ace. The Bruins banged the puck into the Blues' zone and Sanderson skated in and corralled it in the corner. When he looked up, Bobby Orr was barrelling in from the point, calling for the puck. Sanderson laid a perfect pass onto his stick. Noel Picard, the Blues' brawny defenceman, up-ended Orr, figuring he'd snuffed out a scoring chance. But there were times when Orr was unstoppable, and this was one of them. As Orr sailed through the air, almost as if he'd been pitchforked from the blade of Picard's stick, he whistled a shot past Glenn Hall. In an instant the game—and the season—was over.

"Our line didn't even get on the ice in the overtime," said Espo. "That photo of Orr flying through the air has been printed and reprinted a million times. And even though Sanderson didn't score the winner, everybody remembers him setting it up.

"And winning the Cup was the ultimate. For the next three or four years we were top dogs in Boston—more popular than the Red Sox."

The Blues were forced to resign themselves to a pitiful 0–12 record in final appearances. In the two previous finals against Montreal, the Blues, coached by Scotty Bowman, had also been unable to win a single game. No one was predicting at the time that Bowman would one day become the winningest coach in Stanley Cup history.

When Orr scored, Esposito remembers leaping off the bench and catching his skate blade on the dasher. He fell head first on the ice and gashed his chin.

"Orr was mobbed by all of us," Espo recalls. "Then he did something I'll never forget. He sought Ted Green in the crowd and brought him out on the ice. Green was our toughest defenceman, but he'd been partially paralyzed after a violent stick-swinging incident early in the season and we all feared he'd never play again. It was so emotional we all began to cry.

"Some of us pleaded with the NHL to have Teddy's name engraved on the Stanley Cup even though he did not play a game that season. And they did it.

"After a madhouse celebration in the dressing room, we began to party. We partied all night, and a day or two later the city of Boston held a parade for us. Musta been a million people there to honour us. We were all hung over and I remember girls coming up to our car and showing their breasts. It was wild.

"After the parade we were herded onto a stage where Mayor Kevin White made a nice speech. But in the middle of it, Pie McKenzie grabbed a pitcher of beer and poured it over the mayor's head.

"Then there was more partying, and I remember waking up on my front lawn with the Stanley Cup in my arms. Don't ask me how that happened."

Esposito claims he didn't blossom as a hockey player until he reached Boston. "I was traded to the Bruins by Chicago in 1967," he says. "I'd had some success with the Blackhawks—setting up goals for Bobby Hull—but when I scored zero points in the '67 playoffs, the Hawks dealt me off. What a good move that turned out to be—for me and the Bruins."

Espo would go on to score 459 goals as a Bruin, including a 76-goal, 76-assist season in 1970–71.

Orr and Esposito each set two NHL playoff records in 1970. Orr scored nine playoff goals, breaking the previous mark of five set by defenceman Earl Seibert of Chicago in 1938. His 20 points shattered Tim Horton's mark of 16 points by a defenceman in 1962. Esposito's 13 goals beat the previous mark of 12, shared by Rocket Richard and Jean Beliveau of the Canadiens. Espo's 27 points erased the previous record of 21 set by Chicago's Stan Mikita in 1962.

That season, Orr became the first defenceman to win an NHL scoring championship and the Art Ross Trophy, a feat no one thought possible. He added the Norris Trophy and the Hart Trophy and, following the playoffs, was named winner of the Conn Smythe Trophy. No player had ever won four major trophies in one season.

Orr's 120 points during the regular season were more than twice as many as any other defenceman had scored in a single season in league history.

Orr, Espo, and the Bruins were back two years later, facing the New York Rangers in the Stanley Cup finals. Skating on a gimpy knee, Orr dominated again. Boston captured the first two games on home ice, the Rangers fought back with a 5–2 win in game three, but Orr collected a pair of goals and an assist in the Bruins' 3–1 victory in game four. The Rangers came back again with a win but Orr scored a goal and assisted on another as Gerry Cheevers racked up a 3–0 shutout in game six. A huge crowd greeted the Cup holders at Logan Airport when they returned to Boston.

There was an oddity to the Bruin's 1972 capture of the Cup. No player was more thrilled to be part of the Cup celebration than forward Chris Hayes. Never heard of Hayes? His is one of the least-known names on the Stanley Cup. And here's why.

Hayes never played a regular-season game in the NHL. His name does not appear in *Total Hockey*, the encyclopedia listing every NHL player. You could look it up. But he did get on the ice for a few seconds in one of the Bruins' playoff games. That makes him one of the most obscure guys ever to appear in the Stanley Cup playoffs.

Born in Rouyn, Quebec, in 1946, Hayes played his junior hockey with the Oshawa Generals from 1964 to 1967, where he was a teammate of Bobby Orr for two seasons. A left winger, he scored a mere 19 goals over three seasons as a General and opted for college hockey at Loyola in Quebec when the pro teams ignored him.

At Loyola, he blossomed, averaging two points per game, and in 1971, perhaps at Orr's urging, the Bruins signed him as a free agent and sent him to their farm club in Oklahoma City. There he collected 53 points in 72 games, which prompted the Bruins to give him the chance of a lifetime: a roster spot in the Stanley Cup playoffs. He was called up for one game, didn't figure in the scoring, and never played another game for the Bruins.

But the few moments he played as a member of the 1972 Stanley Cup champions made him eligible to have his name engraved on the Stanley Cup.

But hold on! Here's another bizarre bit of trivia. There's another former Bruin whose name is on the Cup, and there's less reason for it to be there than the name of Hayes. This former goalie absolutely did nothing to earn the honour. Goalie Hal Winkler is the imposter. Winkler, who retired from the Bruins in 1928 after compiling an impressive 1.51 goals-against average (still a Boston record) and 15 shutouts. The following season, Winkler didn't play a single minute for the Bruins. Even so, he was listed as the team's sub-goalie in 1929, when the names of the champion Bruins were engraved on the Cup. Why was Winkler's name included? The Bruins added his name because, as one historian put it, he was "such a popular fellow."

Flyers Win Back to Back

Nobody thought the Philadelphia Flyers would upset the Boston Bruins in the 1974 Stanley Cup finals. The Flyers were an expansion team, born in 1967, and as they matured they were condemned by purists as "thugs and backstabbers." During the regular season, the Flyers had spent 1,750 minutes in penalty boxes around the league. No other team had topped 1,400 minutes.

And in the finals, they'd be facing one of the highest-scoring teams in NHL history. At the end of the regular season, the Bruins could point with pride to the fact that the top four scorers in the league all wore Boston colours: Phil Esposito (145 points), Bobby Orr (122), Ken Hodge (105), and Wayne Cashman (89). Flyers captain Bobby Clarke was the only Philadelphian among the league's top ten point getters. But Clarke provided his team with more than points. He was an inspirational leader, and with his long, curly hair and gap-toothed grin, he was the darling of the Philadelphia crowd.

Ted Lindsay, Tim Ryan, and I covered the playoffs on NBC in 1974. We agreed that the Flyers were underdogs, but we also agreed that with Bernie Parent in goal, and with Clarke pushing his mates to "arrive at the net in ill humour," their presence would make a huge difference when the two teams clashed in the finals.

And it did. It also helped to have venerable Kate Smith, enticed by a $5,000 fee, to tiptoe onto the ice prior to the game and warble "God Bless America," pumping up the Flyers and their fans.

When Parent shut out the Bruins 1–0 in game six of the finals on home ice at the Spectrum, the Flyers—without a single player who'd ever experienced the joy of a Stanley Cup victory before—became the first expansion team to capture the Stanley Cup.

Like all champions over the years, Parent wanted to celebrate the win—and his shutout—by parading the Cup around the Spectrum. But he never got a chance. Flyer fans leaped onto the ice and mobbed their heroes. In all the confusion, Parent didn't find out he'd been awarded the Conn Smythe Trophy as the playoff MVP until he reached the team's dressing room.

Phil Esposito paid tribute to the Flyers' key performers. "Bernie Parent was super," he said. "And Clarke never stopped."

"On the day following our big win," Parent recalls," a crowd estimated at a couple of million people turned out to honour us. I looked out over Independence Mall and could see nothing but wall-to-wall people."

Parent found a unique way to show his appreciation for the coaching genius of Fred "The Fog" Shero. When *Sport* magazine handed Bernie the keys to a new car as the playoff MVP, he placed the keys in Shero's hands.

"Freddie deserved it," Parent said. "I remember he said to me, 'Your wife is going to kill you for giving me this car.' I just laughed."

A year later, in the finals again, this time against Buffalo, Parent went from playing for "The Fog" to playing *in* the fog.

Game three in the series should have been postponed. But greed—and TV scheduling—always wins out in these situations. By game time, a blanket of fog filled Buffalo's antiquated Memorial Auditorium. The Flyers had won the first two games at the Spectrum, but the Sabres, dressed in white, used the fog to their advantage and prevailed 5–4 in overtime. Ted Lindsay had played in and seen a thousand games. He'd seen fog over the ice before. But never like that. Play was halted every few minutes while players and college kids waving white sheets skated around the ice, trying to circulate air and dissipate the fog in the non-air-conditioned building. It's a wonder several stars weren't hurt that day, accidentally crashing into each other.

"Trying to stop shots from Buffalo's French Connection Line of Gilbert Perreault, Richard Martin and Rene Robert was almost impossible," Parent said. "They wore white jerseys and their shots coming from out of the fog were enough to put me in a mental institution. There has never been a playoff game in history like that one. Rene Robert's overtime goal won it for the Sabres 5–4."

Parent ended the series in the sixth game, played in Buffalo under normal conditions. When he shut out the Sabres 2–0, he finally got a chance to parade the Stanley Cup around the arena—the Buffalo arena.

"The Buffalo fans even chanted my name—'Bern-ie! Bern-ie!'—just like the Flyers fans did back home. That was nice of them."

In two seasons, Parent had compiled two series-winning shutouts and collected two Stanley Cups and two Conn Smythe Trophies. "Hockey doesn't get much better than that," he said.

When the Flyers returned from Buffalo, a much bigger parade awaited them.

"We had been up most of the night celebrating," Parent recalls. "We'd consumed a lot of beer on the flight back. Now we're on flat-bed trucks, and of course there were no johns on board. Finally, I couldn't hold it any longer, so a big policeman handcuffed himself to me and we ran and knocked on somebody's door. The guy's name was Peter Chille and he said, 'Bernie, come on in, it's an honour. The bathroom's down the hall.' Some writer said that was the most publicized leak in hockey history."

Parent and Clarke enjoyed Hall of Fame careers in Philadelphia.

Clarke had enjoyed a hero's welcome previously. In 1972, he was a pivotal figure on Team Canada in a breathtaking series against the Soviets, won on Paul Henderson's goal in the dying seconds of game eight.

Clarke fans were everywhere. But he had his detractors, especially after he sent the great Soviet player Valery Kharlamov to the sidelines with a slash to the ankle.

"I am convinced he was told to take me out of the series," Kharlamov would say. "I looked into his angry eyes and saw the stick he wielded like a sword."

Years after the event, Paul Henderson would turn on Clarke.

"To me, that was the low point of the series. If Clarke hits him with a body check and takes him out, that's fair and square. To go out and deliberately try to take someone out, there's no sportsmanship in that."

As general manager of the Flyers over the seasons (until he was fired in 2006), Clarke has felt the heat of criticism that was foreign to him as a player. He has been ripped for his degradation of Eric Lindros, for his insensitive firing of Roger Neilson at a time when his popular coach was battling cancer, and always for flaunting his friendship with Alan Eagleson, the disgraced former head of the NHL Players' Association.

Most former NHL players sizzled at Clarke's refusal to side with them in their concerted efforts to oust Eagleson from his NHLPA director's post. Eventually, Eagleson was convicted of fraud, essentially stealing money from the players who trusted him, and served time in jail.

In a recent book, *The Power of Two*, written by Carl Brewer's partner Susan Foster, Brewer is scornful of Clarke.

"Bobby Clarke does not come to the table with clean hands. Leadership? Pshaw! Does a leader of men sell out his teammates? Bobby Clarke betrayed all of the players who fought his battles and gave him the courage to play hockey.

"In essence, Bobby Clarke is a gutless *bleep*!"

The aura surrounding Clarke in his heyday, when he led the Flyers to a pair of Stanley Cups, faded away during his career as a manager.

Too bad. For he was the golden boy of hockey back in 1974 and '75.

During that era, your author was a host-interviewer on the NBC hockey telecasts. And one afternoon, I realized a lifelong dream—to be out on the ice in the middle of a Stanley Cup playoff game. I just wished I'd been there as a player!

Game four of a bitter playoff series between the New York Rangers and the Philadelphia Flyers was played at Madison Square Garden in New York. It was a game New York would win by a 2–1 score. But not before a popular Flyer was tragically injured by a flying puck.

Philadelphia's outstanding defenceman Barry Ashbee was struck in the eye by a Dale Rolfe shot and fell to the ice, writhing in pain. At that moment, I was a few feet away, standing at rinkside with a wireless microphone in my hand, preparing to interview a player during the intermission.

Suddenly, the gates flew open in front of me. The doctors attending Ashbee had called for a stretcher. Impulsively, I started out onto the ice with the stretcher-bearers, intending to interview linesman Matt Pavelich (if possible) about Ashbee's condition. When I passed the Rangers' bench, defenceman Brad Park looked at me in surprise. He called out, "Hey, McFarlane, you're not supposed to be on the ice."

I said, "I know, Brad." But I kept on going.

I pushed my microphone in front of Pavelich and he gave me a firsthand account of Ashbee's injury, which turned out to be much more serious than either of us realized at that moment. Ashbee lost the sight in his eye that afternoon and never played hockey again. Three years later, he was stricken with leukemia and passed away within weeks of being diagnosed with the disease.

He played in only 28 playoff games and never scored a post-season goal. But Philadelphians loved him for his tenacious play. His jersey number, 4, was retired and the Barry Ashbee Trophy was inaugurated, awarded to the Flyer's top defenceman after each season.

As for my bold journey onto Stanley Cup ice that spring day in New York, it did not go unnoticed. A few days later, I passed NHL president Clarence Campbell walking along one of the corridors at Madison Square Garden. He greeted me with a gruff hello and walked on. Then he turned suddenly and called back.

"Brian!"

"Yes, sir?"

"Don't ever do that again."

"What's that, Mr. Campbell?" I said innocently.

"Don't go on the ice ever again. Understand?"

"Yes, sir."

I should have said to him, "Why just me, Mr. Campbell? I see photographers jump on the ice all the time, during times like the Ashbee incident."

Perhaps I should claim some credit for a new edict from NHL headquarters. From that day on, broadcasters *and* photographers were issued strict orders to stay off the ice.

Four Straight for Scotty's Habs

From 1976 through 1979, Scotty Bowman's Montreal Canadiens were all but invincible during the regular season and throughout the playoffs, winning four consecutive Stanley Cups and establishing a record for consistency that has never been matched.

Let's look at Montreal's regular-season stats for that era:

Season	Wins	Losses	Ties
1975–76	58	11	11
1976–77	60	8	12
1977–78	59	10	11
1978–79	52	17	11

In the playoffs over those four seasons, the Habs were almost flawless. In 1976, they won the Cup in 13 games, losing only once. In 1977, they won 12 playoff games and lost only two. In 1978 they won 12 and lost three, and in 1979, they retained the Stanley Cup with a mark of 12 and four. Over the four seasons, their playoff record was 48–10.

They might have won a record-tying fifth consecutive Cup if Ken Dryden hadn't retired, if Scotty Bowman hadn't resigned to take over as GM and coach in Buffalo, if Jacques Lemaire hadn't left to play hockey in Switzerland, and if Yvan Cournoyer hadn't been forced to retire because of back problems.

Bob Gainey suggests that Sam Pollock's decision to step down as GM was another major factor in the Habs' decline. "It was a great run, but you could see some cracks developing," he said. "A few of our guys appeared to be a bit spoiled by our success. And the competition was getting stronger each season."

The Habs remained strong after 1979, but no longer dominant. And there was another team on the rise—the New York Islanders. In 1980, the Isles won the first of *their* four consecutive Cups.

As powerful as the Habs were during the late '70s, with a little more persuasion—and luck—they might have been unbeatable. Bill Torrey, GM of the expansion New York Islanders, drooled over Sam Pollock's offer of several NHL-calibre players in return for the Islanders' top draft choice—Denis Potvin. Torrey ultimately said no, but he was tempted to make the swap.

Later, the Habs had a chance to draft a junior star who resided in their own back yard: Mike Bossy. Scotty Bowman urged Pollock to grab Bossy. But the Montreal scouts questioned Bossy's courage. Sam opted to draft Mark Napier instead. Bossy was taken by the Islanders and scored 50 goals or more for the next nine seasons for a career total of 573.

By the mid-'70s, Bowman knew he had something special—a squad that was developing into one of the greatest teams ever. He had a superb goalie in Dryden. He had three defencemen—Serge Savard, Guy Lapointe, and Larry Robinson—who made life miserable for every opposing forward. He had The Flower, Guy Lafleur, who was simply brilliant, compiling five straight 100-point seasons. Bob Gainey was the best defensive forward in the NHL. Doug Jarvis, not far behind, won almost every faceoff. Snipers Yvan Cournoyer, Steve Shutt, Jaques Lemaire, Doug Risebrough, Rejean Houle, and others made sure the Habs came up with 300 or more goals every season.

Bowman had such an abundance of talent he would switch lines to his heart's content, sit out players who malingered or annoyed him—infuriating some of his stars, delighting others who were given a chance.

Bowman was unpredictable, quirky, critical. Players would say nasty things about him behind his back, but most agreed he knew how to control a game. He always seemed to make the right moves. He was a winner.

The Habs began their streak with a four-game sweep of the Philadelphia Flyers in 1976. The Habs used speed and skill to whip the Flyers, who had relied on toughness and intimidation to capture back-to-back Stanley Cups in '74 and '75.

Cournoyer will never forget the night of May 16, 1976, at the Spectrum in Philadelphia. "I've never seen our team so high. We couldn't stand still—even for the national anthem," he told my *Hockey Night in Canada* colleague Dick Irvin. "We were skating around tapping each other with our sticks and saying 'Let's go! Let's go!' We had the Flyers on the ropes, down three-nothing. We wanted to create an example—that you don't have to be big and tough, and fight all the time, to win the Stanley Cup. We beat them 5–3."

The Habs won despite Kate Smith, who was brought in to sing "God Bless America." When Kate sang, the Flyers usually won—her record was 47–4–1.

Oddly enough, Guy Lafleur, who scored the winning goal that night, could not be found after the game. The NHL's top scorer was not seen sipping Champagne from the Stanley Cup. He was not heard talking into reporter's microphones. He had disappeared. Only after the dressing room cleared did trainer Eddie Pelchak solve the mystery. He opened a small door next to the shower room and there was Lafleur, perched on a stool, sipping a soft drink and staring into space. It had been a stressful playoff run. Lafleur had received a kidnap threat and had been under constant guard by police. His wife and children had been evacuated from their home. His playoff performances had been spotty. Only during the finals did he learn the would-be kidnappers had been caught and charged.

"What a relief!" Lafleur said. "I was still in shock."

Perhaps that explained why he sought the solitude of a broom closet over a wild dressing-room celebration and endless questions from reporters.

The Habs followed up with a four-game sweep of the Bruins in '77, a four-games-to-two win over the Bruins in '78, and a four-games-to-one triumph over the Rangers in '79. One of Guy Lafleur's best-remembered goals was a tying goal against Don Cherry's Bruins in '79 at the Forum. The Bruins, leading by a goal with time running out, had been caught with too many men on the ice late in game seven. Lafleur's blistering shot beat goalie Gilles Gilbert to tie the score, and the Habs won it in overtime.

Years later, I asked Steve Shutt if he knew the Boston player who jumped on the ice and caused the penalty that was so costly to the Bruins. He said, "What the deal was, Cherry wanted Don Marcotte, his best checker, on the ice whenever Lafleur was out there. Now, Cherry had called up a line, and just as they were going over the boards, Lafleur came on for us, and instinctively, Marcotte jumped on to shadow him. But three other Bruins had just leaped on, so I'm sure that Marcotte was the extra guy on the ice."

The following spring, the Canadiens' reign came to an end when the upstart Minnesota North Stars dethroned them in seven games in a quarter-final series.

Long after he retired, Murray Wilson, who played with the Habs from 1972 through 1978, told me an amazing story about a flight from Detroit to Montreal that almost ended in disaster.

"I don't recall the year, but it was during one of our best seasons," he says. "We were flying over London, Ontario, in an old Fairchild F-27 when one engine blew out, spewing flames and smoke along the wing. Smoke filled the plane, and in seconds it heeled over and headed straight for the ground. We were terrified, certain we were all about to be killed. Miraculously, the pilot pulled the plane out of its dive, but not before we'd plunged several thousand feet. He made an emergency landing in London, and we couldn't get off that plane fast enough. One of the great teams in history was that close to being wiped out."

Dryden likes to tell a story about the final seconds of the 1979 playoff season.

"I had decided to retire. I knew that it was my last game. With a few seconds to play we were leading the Rangers 4–1 and I caught the eye of my wife,

Linda, in the crowd. She knew it was my swan song, too. I was going to leave with my name on six Stanley Cups and as the seconds slipped away in the final game, a Ranger player—I believe it was Eddie Johnstone—fired the puck in along the boards. It squirted in behind my net and I moved quickly to trap it there. That's when I heard the final buzzer and I knew another Cup was ours and my career was over. I stood there a moment with the puck in my hand—a lovely souvenir of a special occasion, my final game. Then, Matt Pavelich, the linesman, came over to me and said, 'Ken, can I have the puck? Can I have the puck? This is my final game as an official.'

"I said, 'Matt, it's my last game, too. I'd like to keep the puck.'

"But when I looked into his eyes and saw how much that puck meant to him, and when I thought of how many more years he'd been in the league than I had, I turned my glove over and let the puck drop into his hand."

Lanny McDonald's Biggest Thrills

Lanny McDonald, one of the most popular players ever to play in the NHL, enjoyed two huge playoff thrills in his Hall of Fame career—and they took place 11 years apart.

His first was a game-winning goal in overtime against the Islanders in 1978. He was a key member of the Toronto Maple Leafs back then, along with Darryl Sittler, Tiger Williams, Borje Salming, Ian Turnbull, and goalie Mike Palmateer. A quarterfinal series with the Isles came down to the seventh game on Long Island. The Leafs, coached by rookie mentor Roger Neilson, were decided underdogs against Bryan Trottier, Mike Bossy, Denis Potvin, and company. Believe me, there were a few thousand "nervous Nellies" biting their nails in the Nassau County Coliseum when the final game went to overtime.

The late Dan Kelly and I were in the broadcast booth.

At 4:13 of the first extra period, McDonald trapped a misguided pass at the Islanders blue line. The puck dropped at his feet and he took a few swift strides through open ice toward goaltender Chico Resch. McDonald could wrist a shot with the best of them, but for some reason the shot he put by Resch in OT was a half-speed drive, almost a floater. But it found the back of the net. That's all that counted, and the Leafs rejoiced. Even though the Leafs went on to bow to the Canadiens in the next round, McDonald's marker is recalled as one of the few bright moments in that abysmal era of Leaf hockey, presided over by team owner Harold Ballard.

"I was hurting that night," McDonald recalls. "I wore a football-type shield to protect a broken nose. And I played despite a broken wrist I suffered in a previous series with Los Angeles. But I don't remember feeling any pain at all when that puck floated past Chico Resch. I remember being so shocked I had to ask myself, 'Is it really over?' Then I saw my teammates going nuts over at the bench and knew we'd done it.

"That was the biggest moment of my career until I wound up on a Cup-winning team in Calgary almost a dozen years later," he adds, his eyes gleaming. "No [visiting] team had ever won a deciding game for the Stanley Cup at the Montreal Forum. That was a huge mental hurdle the Flames had to deal with. We were leading the series three games to two and there's no way we wanted to let them back in and force a seventh game back in Calgary."

The game was tied 1–1 in the second period when McDonald was sentenced to two minutes in the penalty box. He had grown a full reddish beard to complement his famous bushy mustache, and when his penalty expired, Lady Luck left the box with him. He stepped out just in time to take a hard pass from Joe Nieuwendyk. Perhaps it was the beard that caught Nieuwendyk's eye. McDonald raced in on goal and fired a bullet past Patrick Roy in the Montreal goal. His goal proved to be the winner, and his biggest ever in hockey. Teammate Doug Gilmour added two more for the Flames, and the lengthy jinx afflicting visiting teams in deciding games at the Forum was finally snapped.

"That goal was by far the best memory I have of my career," McDonald says today. "Because it helped to bring us the Stanley Cup. But that goal in overtime against the Islanders in '78 is a pretty special memory, too."

Chico Resch laughed when he was told of McDonald's remarks.

"Lanny's goal in '78 was a crushing blow for the Islanders," said Resch. "He drove a stake through our hearts with that goal. Do you know we faced each other again in a charity game in Denver a few months ago? It was '78 all over again. Here he comes, racing in on me. And he shoots the damn puck 15 feet wide of the net. Why didn't he do that the first time when it really meant something?"

Who Stole the Cup?

You never know when you are going to hear a fascinating Stanley Cup story. This one came straight from the lips of Guy Lafleur.

In June of 1979, the Canadian Society of New York held a hockey banquet. I was there as MC for the event, and several of the recently crowned Stanley Cup champion Montreal Canadiens were at the head table. With microphone in hand, I interviewed each one, and when I came to Guy Lafleur, he treated the audience to a caper he'd concocted the day after the Habs had won the Cup, their fourth in a row. Incidentally, Lafleur and Jacques Lemaire led all playoff scorers with 23 points in 16 games and were two of the most heralded Habs during the mammoth victory parade through downtown Montreal.

Lafleur's story went like this:

> There was great joy in Montreal after we captured another Stanley Cup, beating the Rangers in five games in the final series.·
>
> There was a huge victory party at Toe Blake's tavern followed by another party at Henri Richard's tavern. All the while, Canadiens publicity man Claude Mouton was

keeping a close eye on the Stanley Cup, keeping it locked in the trunk of his car whenever it was not on display or being filled with Champagne.

But he didn't watch it closely enough, I guess. He wandered off somewhere and a few of us moved his car. Then we broke into the trunk and took the Cup—just to play a little joke on Mouton. But then I thought, why not take this lovely Cup back home to Thurso, Quebec, where my parents live? Won't they be surprised? So I slipped the Stanley Cup into the trunk of my car and drove home to Thurso.

My father couldn't believe it when I took the Cup out of my car and placed it on the lawn in front of his house. He called all his friends and said, "Come see the Cup! Come see the Cup!" People came from everywhere to look at it, to touch it, and to be photographed next to it. There was never a sight like that in Thurso.

We didn't have any Champagne to put in the Cup, but my son Martin filled it with water from the garden hose, and I guess some of the people drank that. I remember telling Martin, "Remember, this is the great Stanley Cup. You must always treat it with respect."

Meanwhile, back in Montreal, Claude Mouton was frantic with worry. He told some of my teammates, "Somebody has stolen the Stanley Cup. They took it right out of the trunk of my car. Who would do such a thing?"

And somebody said, "Well, perhaps it was Guy Lafleur? He left town in a big hurry. Did you not notice?"

Mouton shook his head. "No, it was not Lafleur," he said. "Guy is too quiet. That rascal Guy Lapointe might have done it. But not Lafleur. He would never do such a thing."

In Thurso, I began to get worried. What if something happens to the Cup while it's here with me? What if it gets damaged or stolen? Now I was almost as concerned about the Cup as Claude Mouton. So I jumped in my car and took the Cup back to Montreal. But I didn't give it to Mouton. I didn't want him to learn that I was the culprit. So I left it at the Canadiens' office at the Montreal Forum. Then I got out of town again before Mouton found me. By then he probably would have throttled me.

The audience howled at Lafleur's story. And I had it on my tape recorder. In his very own words.

I was determined to turn it over to my favourite radio station in Toronto when I arrived back the next day. It's a story well worth sharing, I thought.

But when I got back to Toronto, I discovered that Guy's story of the stolen Cup was on every radio station—and in every newspaper.

It wasn't the first time that weekend that Guy Lafleur regaled us with a Stanley Cup story. At a reception the evening before the Canadian Society Dinner, at which there were 47 Stanley Cups represented at the table, he talked about first joining the Canadiens.

When I first played with Montreal for the 1971–72 season, I was in awe of established stars like Jean Beliveau, Henri Richard, and Frank Mahovlich.

All of these great men had been on Stanley Cup teams many times and I wondered if there would be any Cups left for me to win.

I didn't have to wait very long for an answer. In 1973, the Canadiens met the Chicago Blackhawks in the Stanley Cup finals. NBC covered the finals that season and billed game four as "a battle between two great goaltenders—Ken Dryden and Tony Esposito." Neither netminder showed

179

much greatness that day. Both were so shaky, the final score was 8–7 for Chicago as the teams set a playoff record for goal scoring.

Two days later, at the Chicago Stadium, we won the Stanley Cup, defeating the Hawks 6–4 in another high-scoring affair.

It was my first Stanley Cup, and I was so thrilled to be on a Cup winner that I mixed some drinks during the post-game celebration—lots of beer and almost as much Champagne.

I don't remember much about the plane ride back to Montreal on our charter. I recall that my teammate, Claude Larose, was laid out on a stretcher because he had suffered a broken leg in the final game. When we landed in Montreal I was so drunk I couldn't get out of my seat. So big Butch Bouchard grabbed Larose and tossed him off the stretcher. Then he picked me up and threw me on it. Poor Claude had to be helped off the plane by some of the guys while I was carried off on a stretcher. I always felt bad about that.

I would get to play on four more Stanley Cup–winning teams with Montreal. But I'll never forget that first one.

Bruins' Blunder Costs Cherry His Job

On the night of May 10, 1979, Don Cherry, the flamboyant coach of the Boston Bruins, thought he was going to have a heart attack. He looked out on the ice of the Montreal Forum and gasped. The Bruins had too many men on the ice.

"My heart pounded," he recalls, wincing. "I longed for a long hook—anything—to get that man off before the officials noticed. But the linesman, John D'Amico, noticed. He threw his arm up and I can still hear the whistle that stopped play. That was almost three decades ago."

The Forum was the scene of a gripping semifinal series between Cherry's Bruins and the Montreal Canadiens. Until the Bruins blundered, the seventh and deciding game was about to end disastrously for the Habs. They trailed by a goal as fans squirmed in their seats and prayed for a miracle. After three straight Cup wins, their beloved Canadiens were less than two minutes away from elimination. A berth in the Stanley Cup finals appeared to be beyond their reach.

If coach Don Cherry's Bruins could hold onto their 4–3 lead over the Montreal Canadiens in the scant few seconds that remained, it would be the Bruins who would meet the New York Rangers in the Stanley Cup finals.

Moments earlier, with 3:59 to play, the Bruins had celebrated a go-ahead goal by slippery Rick Middleton. Then, as the final seconds ticked off the clock, there was momentary confusion at the Boston bench. On a quick line change, an extra Bruin leaped over the boards and the official's whistle shattered Cherry's world.

"I died then," he says. "It was 11:10 p.m."

The Bruins suddenly, shockingly, found themselves playing shorthanded. Cherry knew the incredible gaffe could cost his team the game and the Stanley Cup. Even worse, it could cost him his job.

With just over a minute left on the clock, Guy Lafleur led a rush from inside his own blue line. He flew past centre ice and darted over the Boston blue line. In desperation, he blasted a shot that was perfectly timed, precisely aimed. The puck skimmed past Bruins netminder Gilles Gilbert, who threw his right pad at the puck, then sprawled on his back, arms outflung.

Too late.

The puck caught the far corner of the net. Game tied! There was 1:14 to play.

The old Montreal Forum rocked as Hab fans rejoiced, knowing momentum was now swinging their way. Cherry and the Bruins cursed the hockey fates that had now left them vulnerable.

In overtime, the Bruins, still rattled by their sickening third-period bench error, failed to stop a centring pass from Mario Tremblay to Hab winger Yvon Lambert, who was parked to one side of the Bruins' goal crease. He deflected a shot off the pads of Gilbert and into the open net.

Game over!

Cherry felt like he'd been run over by a bulldozer.

Montreal had won the series and the right to advance against the Rangers, a team that was no match for either of the semifinalists.

Cherry and the Bruins were devastated.

"I knew that night I was a goner," Cherry would say. "Harry Sinden [the Bruins' manager] was looking for any kind of excuse to can me, and having too many men on the ice in a critical situation like that was all that it took. It's been three decades since that night at the Forum, and millions of people must have seen what happened because it seems that every day somebody wants to remind me of it."

Sure enough, Cherry was fired. Or was he? When Don authored a book, *Grapes: A Vintage View of Hockey*, he revealed that he could have kept his job with the Bruins—if he'd promise to get along with Sinden. "You have to realize that Harry is the boss," he was told. "You two have to stop squabbling." Cherry figured that if Sinden didn't get him this time, he'd get him next time. And that Sinden would begin to get rid of Cherry's favourites—players like Rick Smith, Al Secord, and Bobby Schmautz. Cherry said "Thanks, but no thanks" and left his beloved Bruins. Whether he was fired or simply walked away, the Boston media was all over the parting. "IT WAS A MISTAKE," screamed the Boston *Herald*. Writer Joe Fitzgerald said: "I've got a hunch that Harry's mind was made up the first time Cherry told a joke that got a laugh. From the moment Cherry walked onto the center stage at the Garden, Sinden became a forgotten man, and his resentment has been festering for a long, long time."

Cherry's agent, Al Eagleson, negotiated on his behalf with Colorado and Toronto. Shortly after Cherry accepted the Colorado offer, the Leafs came through with more money.

"Take it!" Eagleson hollered.

"I can't," Cherry replied. "Even though I'd love to coach the Leafs."

"Take the Leaf job," Eagleson snorted. "You haven't signed with Colorado, have you?"

"No, but I gave them my word," Cherry stated. "I never go back on my word."

That's the kind of guy Cherry is. He cried over missing out on the Leaf job, but he went on to coach the woeful Colorado Rockies for a couple of seasons and was soon fired from that job, too.

But it all turned out rather well for the man who once claimed he often let his dog, Blue, select his team's starting goaltender. He joined *Hockey Night in Canada*, hired someone from the Liberace School of Tailoring to outfit him in multi-hued jackets, and became the most famous commentator in hockey history. It was my pleasure, for a brief time, to sit next to him on "Coach's Corner". Those were some of the moments I enjoyed most in a lengthy career in hockey broadcasting.

And hey, why isn't Grapes in the media section of the Hockey Hall of Fame? He's been the most watched, most listened to commentator in hockey broadcasting for almost 25 years.

Isles Soar to the Top

When the New York Islanders won four Stanley Cups in a row from 1980 to 1983, they established themselves as one of the greatest hockey clubs of all time.

In 1980, it was Bob Nystrom's overtime goal in game six against Philadelphia that brought the Islanders their first Stanley Cup.

Mike Bossy's 35 playoff points helped bring a second Cup the following spring in a one-sided triumph over Minnesota.

Bossy's brilliance (17 playoff goals) was a key to the Islanders' ouster of the Vancouver Canucks in the 1982 finals. Even "King Richard" Brodeur's outstanding goaltending failed to stop Conn Smythe Trophy winner Bossy and the rest of the Isles, who won in four straight games.

At one point, the prolific Bossy was thrown high in the air by a hard check. While parallel to the ice, looking down, he skillfully managed to get his stick on the puck and hook it into the Vancouver net. I've seen goals scored from all angles, and many were spectacular. But that one by Bossy was very special, very memorable. It left you blinking your eyes in disbelief.

The 1983 final series between the Oilers and the Islanders was billed as a dream matchup: Gretzky and Messier versus Bossy and Trottier. Billy Smith versus Grant Fuhr. Smith held the Oilers to only seven goals and shut out Gretzky completely in the Islanders' stunning four-game sweep. Smith was a worthy winner of the Conn Smythe Trophy. During the four year playoff run, he went 57–13. But the Oilers could not be denied 12 months later, when they ended the Isles' "Drive for Five."

Manager Bill Torrey's Islanders had made an indelible mark on hockey. Few teams in any major sport, starting from scratch, had been able to soar to the top in less than a decade and then repeat as champions over such a long stretch. The only major league franchises to capture four or more consecutive championships had been the New York Yankees (1936–39 and '49–54), the Boston Celtics (1959–66), and the Montreal Canadiens (1956–60 and '76–79).

Since it was illogical to compare the Islanders' streak to that of the Yankees or the Red Sox, and the Edmonton Oilers four-year dynasty had yet to begin, how would the Islanders have fared against the Canadiens?

"I'd love to play either of those famous Montreal teams with a lot of money at stake," Islander manager Torrey once told me. "The game has changed a lot since the mid-'50s when the Habs iced a team loaded with future Hall of Famers.

"They packed most of their firepower into the first two lines, and their third line checked like crazy. They had the Richard brothers—Maurice and Henri—alongside Dickie Moore on the first line. Jean Beliveau and Boom Boom Geoffrion were part of a second line. Doug Harvey and Tom Johnson were on defence, with Jacques Plante in goal. Don't forget coach Toe Blake behind the bench. All of them in the Hall of Fame today."

Torrey grew up not far from the Montreal Forum and remembers that team well.

"The Islanders' answer to Plante and Harvey would be Billy Smith and Dennis Potvin. Mike Bossy's scoring stats are comparable to the Rocket's, and centre Bryan Trottier is in a class with Henri Richard and Beliveau."

Rabid Montreal fans could never accept that the Islanders would be a match for either of the Montreal dynasties.

Veteran hockey writer Red Fisher, when asked about the 1976–79 Canadiens, says, "There was never a troika on the blue line like Guy Lapointe, Larry Robinson, and Serge Savard. Potvin was as good as any one of them, but there was only one Potvin."

Fisher and others will tell you that Montreal's superb defence, bolstered by goaltender Ken Dryden and outstanding forwards like Yvan Cournoyer, Guy Lafleur, Steve Shutt, and Bob Gainey, and with Scotty Bowman coaching, would have been more than a match for Torrey's Islanders.

The 1976–77 edition of the Habs fashioned the best regular-season record in NHL history, going 60–8–12 before cruising through the playoffs with a 12–2 mark.

When told that most experts placed the Islanders third on the list of hockey dynasties, behind the Canadiens of the '50s and the Habs of the '70s, Dennis Potvin was unfazed.

"As far as I'm concerned," he said with a grin, "we're the best hockey team ever to lace on skates."

Manager Bill Torrey (my teammate at St. Lawrence University in the '50s) credits the Islanders' success to the coaching of Al Arbour, who joined the team in 1973. In his first season, stressing defensive play, Arbour improved his young club's performance by 25 points. The following season, the Isles improved by another 32 points. In 1975–76, Arbour's men topped 100 points and continued to do so for five of the next six seasons. The four consecutive Stanley Cups they won is a record for an American team. During their glory years, the Isles put together a string of 19 consecutive playoff series victories—a pro sports record.

Arbour's tally of coaching wins soared until he retired after the 1993–94 season with 781—739 of them with the Islanders. He ranks second to Scotty Bowman (1,244) on the NHL's list of winningest coaches.

Arbour's final win was memorable. At age 75 and in failing health, he was invited back to coach the Islanders one more time. Coach Ted Nolan wanted him to finish with a nice round figure: 1,500 games behind the Isles' bench. On November 3, 2007, Arbour guided the Isles to a 3–2 win over Pittsburgh, earning his 740th victory. That night, he became the oldest man in NHL history to coach a team.

He's always been one of the most popular.

Scotty Bowman on the Cup

Scotty Bowman and I are having breakfast at the Waldorf-Astoria in New York. We are there for the annual Canadian Society of New York hockey banquet. It is 1992, and Scotty's Pittsburgh Penguins have just captured the Stanley Cup, sweeping the Chicago Blackhawks, coached by Mike Keenan. Bowman shared some of his thoughts about the Stanley Cup, a trophy with which he is very familiar. Over the course of his career, he won nine times as a coach with Montreal, Pittsburgh, and Detroit.

> I often read about the fact they call the Stanley Cup a battered old mug. I know that in Montreal in the '70s we could never get near the Cup. It was the Holy Grail of hockey. It seemed there was always a rope around it and we couldn't get close—except maybe to get our photos taken with it as winners.
>
> The one player who started to change all that was Guy Lafleur. He sneaked off with the Cup after our '79 win and took it home to Thurso, Quebec, where his parents lived. It caused quite a sensation. I heard he brought it to someone's house and left it alongside somebody's swimming pool.

Well, the neighbour phoned and said, "Do you know you left the Stanley Cup next to the pool?" Guy's wife was upset and told him, "You get back there and look after the Cup."

I know in our situation—when we won in Pittsburgh—they started out handling it very gracefully. But after that... anything can happen.

Obviously, it has a lot of resiliency. It's been dented and banged around but it always comes back looking great—beautiful.

After both years we won it [in Pittsburgh], it wound up in Mario Lemieux's swimming pool. Phil Bourque stepped back a few feet and heaved it toward the pool. If he'd missed we'd still be picking up the pieces. And the players soon discovered that it doesn't float. It sinks right to the bottom. The first year, they tried to lift it out of the pool, and the bowl on top was perhaps a little weak. The second year, they were smarter. They realized it took two of them to get it out of the pool because it was so heavy. They found out it holds a lot of water, and if they brought it up upside down, the water pours out of it. I guess it was none the worse for wear.

Over the years, there's been a lot of controversy over how you get your name on the Cup. In the '70s, we had a player in Montreal, Don Awrey, who broke his leg just before the playoffs. He missed out because back then you had to play at least one game in the final series to be eligible. Then they changed it to one playoff game. Now I believe it's if you've played 40 regular-season games for the winning team. Or, if you were on the team roster at the trading deadline you can qualify, providing, of course, the winning team submits a list and there's room for your name. Remember, the owners and managers want to see their names on the Cup, too.

When we won in Pittsburgh in '91, some of our scouts were disappointed. There was no room for them. And yet—get this—our strength conditioning coach, who nobody really knows, got his name on the Cup, with "strength conditioning coach" engraved after it. His title and name took up a whole line.

The first Cup we won in Montreal was in 1973. We won the Cup in May, and our baby was due around that time. When we had a boy, born in June, we decided to name him Stanley. We named him Stanley Glenn—Glenn after Glenn Hall, our goalie in St. Louis. So our newborn son got a real hockey name. When he was young, we always called him Stanley Cup. Now a few years go by, and one day I was in some office—an insurance office per-haps— filling in some forms. Stanley was with me, waiting while I filled in all the family names. When we left, I noticed that Stanley was really glum. I said, "What's wrong, son?" And he said, "Dad, is my name not Stanley Cup anymore?"

I reassured him as best I could. I said, "Son, your name will always be Stanley Cup to us."

A unique thing happened to Stanley in 1992. He was at college at Notre Dame and he took a couple of days off to come to Chicago to see Pittsburgh play the Blackhawks. When we swept the series, after game four, he slipped out on the ice and was part of the victory celebration. That's something he'll never forget.

When Scotty Bowman was a young coach in St. Louis, he was often cri-tiqued by a talkative woman who sat directly behind the Blues' bench. One night, with Detroit leading the Blues 1–0 on a Gordie Howe goal, the woman bellowed at Bowman late in the game, "Pull the goalie, you dummy!"

But there were still five minutes left to play. Bowman ignored the fan, even though she continued to shout, "You dummy coach. Pull the goalie!"

Then, with a minute left on the clock, Bowman yanked his goalie for an extra attacker. Just then, Gordie Howe snagged a loose puck, lifted it high in the air, and it settled squarely in the empty St. Louis net. The Red Wings were seconds away from a 2–0 win and the arena went silent.

Before the ensuing faceoff, Bowman took one last shot from the female fan, "Not *that* goalie, you dummy coach. You should have pulled the *other* goalie."

Bowman was then embarking on a hockey coaching career that would see him capture the game's most coveted trophy, the Stanley Cup, a record nine times. His name is on the Cup three times with Detroit, five times with Montreal, and twice with Pittsburgh.

After his Detroit Red Wings helped him set the record in June, 2002, at his home in Amherst, New York, Bowman decided to share some Stanley Cup magic with his friends and neighbours. He placed the Stanley Cup in his back yard and left a "Come and see the Cup" invitation taped to a hockey stick outside his front door.

At least 800 visitors responded. Cars were parked everywhere.

One of the first on the scene was a young fan with leukemia, 11-year-old Kevin McCorry, who took photos to show all his friends at school.

"Mr. Bowman said there were over 2,200 names on the Stanley Cup," said Kevin. "I'll bet he knows a few hundred of those fellows personally."

While Bowman is universally applauded for his accomplishments, there's at least one bench boss—and a few players—who are loath to praise hockey's winningest coach.

On May 22, 1997, during game four of a bruising playoff series between Detroit and Colorado, Avalanche coach Marc Crawford went ballistic after the Red Wings achieved a 6–0 lead. Crawford lashed out at Bowman verbally, accused him of sending a "bunch of thugs" onto the ice. Crawford tried to scale a glass partition to accost Bowman, but he was restrained by his assistant coaches. Crawford's tantrum cost him a thousand-dollar fine.

A former NHL player who may share Crawford's feelings for Bowman is Dave "Tiger" Williams. In the third game of a 1980 playoff series between Bowman's Buffalo Sabres and the Vancouver Canucks, Williams skated past the Buffalo bench and suddenly Bowman went flying backwards. He landed flat on his back, out cold and at the feet of his astonished players. Later, he accused Williams of hitting him with "a real two-hander over the head."

After the contest, Williams was questioned. "Gee," he said, his rugged face the picture of innocence, "I don't remember hitting Bowman. Of course, when he leans over the boards like he does, accidents may happen…"

Brian O'Neill, executive vice-president of the NHL, examined tapes of the game and saw enough evidence to support Bowman's claim. He suspended Williams for one game.

After a record 30 years behind NHL benches, Bowman amassed a record 1,244 victories.

What a career!

I worked with Scotty often on *Hockey Night in Canada* and was fascinated by his total focus on the game and the anecdotes he would share with me.

"My first coaching job was in 1954. I was 21 and I coached a Junior B team in Montreal. They paid me $250 for the season.

"When I was a high school kid, I had a friend whose folks owned a cleaners. That's where the Canadiens sent their embroidered jackets for cleaning. My friend and I 'borrowed' two of the jackets off the cleaning rack one day and wore them to the school dance. We thought we were so cool, wearing jackets with the Habs logo on the pocket.

"My chances to become a pro player ended on March 7, 1952, when Jean-Guy Talbot hit me over the head in a junior game. He cut me for 42 stitches. I had a lot of headaches and my vision was blurred. But I don't have a metal plate in my head, as has often been reported. I was never the same player after that.

"Did you know I collect hockey cards? I was smart. I bought 50 Brett Hull rookie cards.

"Glen Sather did something I wish I'd thought of. He was angry because the players' bench in Colorado was too small. Visiting players struggled to get over the boards on line changes there. So Sather had carpenters make a similar bench in Edmonton when the Oilers played the Avalanche in the playoffs one year. He gave the Avalanche a dose of their own medicine.

Goalie Ken Dryden, writing about Bowman in his fascinating book *The Game*, said: "Scotty Bowman is not someone who is easy to like. He does not slap backs, punch arms or grab elbows. He is shy and not very friendly. Abrupt, straightforward and sometimes obnoxious, controversial, but never colourful. He plays favourites. His favourites, while rarely feeling favoured, are those who work and produce for him. He is complex, confusing, misunderstood, unclear in every way but one. He is a brilliant coach, the best of his time."

Dryden once told Dick Irvin: "Players who didn't say a lot of nice things about Scotty at other times, when we'd be in a playoff series against Don Cherry and the Bruins or Fred Shero and the Flyers, they'd be shaking their heads in the dressing room, saying how you just couldn't believe how Scotty had control of the game. He'd have Cherry or Shero doing exactly what he wanted them to do. The players just couldn't believe how he could do that during a game."

In July, 2008, Bowman joined the Chicago Blackhawks as a senior advisor. His son Stan, the Hawks' director of hockey operations, as you now know, is named after the Stanley Cup. With his father's help, he may soon see his name officially engraved on the trophy.

Those Awesome Oilers

There was a time long ago when a team from Edmonton, hopeful of winning the Stanley Cup, strengthened themselves by icing a team of ringers. In 1909, before leaving for Montreal and a two-game series with the Wanderers, the Edmonton club recruited, at great expense, all the best players available. Only one man on the squad, Fred Whitcroft, was an Edmonton native. The others were mercenaries. Even with nine ringers, the Edmonton boys lost the series by a combined score of 10–8.

Decades later, in the 1980s, manager/coach Glen Sather wasn't seeking ringers when he controlled the destiny of the Edmonton Oilers. Dismissed initially as a journeyman player with minimal front-office skills, Sather quickly made his critics chew on their words. He was busy assembling a core of great young players—Wayne Gretzky, Jari Kurri, Mark Messier, Paul Coffey, Glenn Anderson, Grant Fuhr, and Kevin Lowe. These kids matured as Oilers and soon proved themselves to be a joy to watch and one of the best teams ever. In the '80s, the Oilers were the epitome of hockey excellence.

Canadien and Islander fans may justly brag about their teams' dynasties, but Sather's Oilers fashioned a run of success to rival any other. One edition of the Oilers—the 1987–88 club—has been recognized by *The Sporting News* as one of the top five teams in any sport—from the last 120 years!

The Oilers started out as refugees from the World Hockey Association. Led by a kid named Gretzky, a youth who was labelled "too small, too slow, too fragile" to become a presence in the NHL, they shot to prominence with a stunning sweep of the Montreal Canadiens in a 1981 playoff series—the year the Islanders won the Cup. Montreal coach Claude Ruel was so devastated by the upset that he resigned, vowing never to coach again.

The Oilers encountered a setback in 1982. In one of the most stunning playoff upsets in Stanley Cup history, the lowly Los Angeles Kings eliminated the high-flying Oilers in a best-of-five playoff series.

On paper, the Kings didn't have a chance. During the regular season, the Oilers had compiled 111 points to the Kings' meagre 63. The Oilers had won 48 games, the Kings a mere 24. The Oilers had scored an NHL record 417 goals (83 more than L.A.), with Wayne Gretzky figuring in over half of them. It was Gretzky's finest season. He shattered Phil Esposito's record for goals (76) with 92, and set new records for assists (120) and total points (212).

The Kings didn't care about all that. They won the opener of the series by the remarkable score of 10–8. That night, the teams combined to set an NHL record for total goals in a playoff game. Los Angeles followed up with a 3–2 victory over Gretzky, Coffey, Fuhr, and company. In game three, the Oilers held a five-goal lead. Then they blew it and lost to the Kings in overtime.

Terry Jones, a reporter for the *Edmonton Journal*, was apoplectic over the demise of the team he covered. He wrote, "From today until they've won a playoff series again, the Oilers are weak-kneed wimps who thought they were God's gift to the NHL but found out they were nothing but adolescent, front-running, good-time Charlies who couldn't handle any adversity."

Ouch!

Two years later, the Oilers made it to the Cup finals, but still lacking post-season experience, were swept by the powerful Islanders.

Lessons learned, in 1984 they soared to the finals again, sending the Islanders reeling with a 4–1 series win. Gretzky provided the spark in the fifth game by scoring twice and assisting on another goal. Mark Messier was awarded the Conn Smythe Trophy as playoff MVP, but he pushed the trophy aside and told reporters, "Gretz made a great little speech before the game. He told us all the individual trophies he'd won could never compare with winning the Stanley Cup. That got us all fired up."

In 1985, the Oilers were back in the finals and facing a challenge from the Philadelphia Flyers. The Flyers rolled to a 4–1 victory in game one, but failed to capture another game. When the Oilers blasted the Flyers 8–3 in game five, they set a playoff record for most goals in a deciding game.

"This might be the start of a dynasty," Gretzky told us. He had just won the Smythe Trophy and established a playoff record for most points in a playoff year with 47 (17 goals, 30 assists in 18 games).

We all agreed with Gretz about that dynasty thing.

And it almost was the start of one.

But an aberration, a horrific glitch, derailed the Oilers in the '86 Smythe Division finals. It was a Battle of Alberta between the Oilers and the Flames. Who can forget the shocking ending? Third period, game tied 2–2. The Flames' Perry Berezan shoots the puck into the Oiler zone. Young defenceman Steve Smith corrals it, then juggles the disc beside his own net. He commits an incredible gaffe with his errant pass. Millions watching on *Hockey Night in Canada* gasp as the puck glances off Grant Fuhr's pads, drifts over the goal line and into the Oiler net. Flames win, 3–2. There's never been a post-season goal—or a playoff moment of any description—as shocking as that one. One can only imagine how Smith felt—and still feels—when he thinks of that agonizing moment.

"I'll live with it forever," Smith says, two decades later.

Smith's eyes were still watering as he watched the Montreal Canadiens—with rookie Patrick Roy as MVP—defeat the Flames for the Cup that season.

But his tears of despair turned to tears of joy one year later, in 1987. In the finals, the Oilers ousted the Flyers and their hot goaltender, Ron Hextall, to capture their third Cup in four years. The first player Wayne Gretzky handed the Cup to during the Oilers' victory lap was Steve Smith.

There was an oddity associated with that final series. Flyer goalie Ron

Hextall, wielding a big stick, was suspended for 10 games after game four as punishment for a vicious slash across the legs of Kent Nilsson. Did he sit out? No, the suspension was postponed until the following season. It didn't make sense. Hextall was rewarded with the Conn Smythe Trophy, becoming only the fourth player (Roger Crozier, Glenn Hall, Reg Leach, and Jean-Sebastien Giguere being the others) to win the trophy while playing for a losing team. With luck, he might have captured a Stanley Cup ring—while under suspension!

Rocket Richard should have been so lucky in 1955.

What fun it was to be around the Oilers in those days. Chatting with Gretzky about his record seasons, his 92 goals, his three seasons of more than 200 points; with Paul Coffey about his 48 goals and 138 points in 1985–86; with Grant Fuhr about—well, Fuhr never said very much about anything. But his goaltending spoke volumes.

Then came another trip to the finals against Boston in 1988—the blackout series. A power outage at the shabby, outdated Boston Garden ended game four prematurely. The game was replayed in Edmonton two nights later and won by the Oilers to complete a sweep. But the stats from the cancelled game were declared valid, which created some hockey trivia. It means the Bruins' Greg Hawgood can tell his grandkids, "I scored a goal in a playoff game in Boston, and while it counted, it didn't mean a thing."

The Bruins' Rick Middleton might add, "I scored my 100th playoff point in a non-contest. You can look it up."

Gretzky was dominant again with 43 playoff points and another Conn Smythe Trophy. "They should pass the guy around from team to team each year," Boston coach Terry O'Reilly told us.

Wayne Gretzky had a busy off-season in '88, smiling for the cameras on his wedding day on July 16—probably the biggest social event Edmontonians had ever witnessed—and sobbing openly 25 days later after learning he'd been traded to the L.A. Kings for $15 million. There were other players involved, but essentially it was a sale by Peter Pocklington, the cash-strapped owner of the Oilers. Gretzky fans pilloried owner Pocklington, and the deal remains the most talked about trade in hockey history.

Gretzky, in his new duds—and before Kings owner Bruce McNall went to prison—promptly led his new club from 18th position to fourth overall. In a playoff series against the Oilers in 1989, the Kings fell behind 3–1 in games, then stormed back with three straight wins, snuffing out any chance of a third straight Cup for the Alberta boys.

In the finals, the province cheered for another Alberta team—the Flames—as they marched to the Cup, eliminating Montreal right in the Montreal Forum, in Lanny McDonald's final season.

Almost two years after Gretzky left the city, Edmonton fans still blistered Pocklington. But they were pacified somewhat when the Oilers skated their way into the 1990 Cup finals and trampled Boston in five games. Standing out was the magnificent play of Mark Messier, who, at the end, held the Cup aloft and shouted into the TV cameras, "This one's for you, Gretz."

V. Individual Headline-Makers

Neilson's Towel-Waving Part of Stanley Cup Lore

It's hard to believe a simple white towel could trigger such a reaction. I was in the broadcast booth at the mammoth Chicago Stadium on a spring night in 1982 when Roger Neilson raised the towel in a gesture of mock surrender.

But let's go back a month, to the final few days of the 1981–82 season, when our story really begins. There was a game played in Quebec between the Nordiques and the Vancouver Canucks. The fans began heckling Canuck coach Harry Neale, and in moments a scuffle broke out. Neale was peppered with debris and he and his players turned on the howling mob.

When the melee ended, Neale and one of his defencemen, Doug Halward, were suspended for the remaining six games of the season.

Roger Neilson, Neale's assistant coach, stepped in and galvanized the Canucks. They went undefeated for the rest of the season.

Neale was smart enough not to tamper with a winning streak. He ordered Neilson to keep on coaching into the playoffs.

The Canucks swarmed all over Calgary in the first round, winning three straight in the best-of-five series. In the next round, Neilson and the Canucks faced the L.A. Kings, who were coming off a stunning upset over the Edmonton Oilers. Suddenly, inexplicably, the NHL's second-best team had been eliminated from the Stanley Cup hunt by the 17th-place Kings.

The Kings were hot, but they couldn't cope with Roger Neilson's magic and were ousted by the Canucks, four games to one.

On to the third round. Led by Stan Smyl, Tiger Williams, and goaltender "King Richard" Brodeur, the Canucks invaded the ancient Chicago Stadium and emerged with a double-overtime victory over the Blackhawks in game one.

Our *Hockey Night in Canada* crew was there for game two, a 4–1 victory for the Blackhawks. The Canucks came apart in the second period of the game and were dinged with four straight penalties.

Tiger Williams would later accuse referee Bob Myers of making incredibly bad decisions and drawing attention to himself by making a number of cheap calls.

When Myers signalled a fifth penalty to the Canucks, Williams was tempted to protest by "throwin' every friggin' stick in the rack on the ice." But coach Neilson had a better idea. He reached back and grabbed a spare stick. He threw a white towel around the blade and lifted it high in mock surrender, waving it in Myers' face.

Williams and two or three other Canucks followed suit. While Myers fumed, the Chicago mob booed, then laughed.

But Neilson's impulsive protest drew quick support from Vancouver fans watching on television. Towel Power was born.

Williams called Neilson "damn near a genius. That towel waving united us and we were unbeatable in the next three games."

For game three in Vancouver, over 16,000 rabid, white-towel-waving fans cheered themselves hoarse and gleefully watched the Canucks surge ahead in the series.

"It looked like a snowstorm inside the arena," said one commentator.

By the time game four began, the city was awash in white towels. The Canucks rolled to another win.

In the deciding game, played in Chicago, Ron Delorme, a real standup guy, beat the tar out of the Hawks' Paul Mulvey. After that, the Hawks lost their will to fight on.

A million towels and a substitute coach, along with Richard Brodeur's fabulous goaltending, had catapulted the Canucks into their first-ever Stanley Cup finals.

Williams savours the memory. "So we lost in the Stanley Cup finals to the Islanders. They had some great players. The thing is, we fought like hell to get there. We had a lot to be proud of that season."

The Isles seized their third straight Stanley Cup, becoming the first American team to do so.

But even today, the white towels come out in Vancouver when the hometown team needs a visual boost. Neilson is gone, but his towel-waving gesture on that long ago night in Chicago will forever be remembered.

Schoenfeld Blasts Koharski

Tempers run high at playoff time, and coaches sometimes say things they later regret. Then again, perhaps they don't regret them at all. Especially if they have a habit of throwing barbs at lowly referees, serfs on skates whose decisions can drive a coach to distraction.

Certainly, the opinions expressed by New Jersey Devils coach Jim Schoenfeld following a playoff game with the Boston Bruins in 1988 caught the ear of Don Koharski, the zebra who bore the brunt of Schoenfeld's scorn, as well as the collective ear of a nationwide TV audience.

Perhaps you are too young to remember that bizarre night.

Let me tell you about it.

Livid over the refereeing of Koharski after game three of the Wales Conference finals, Schoenfeld accosted Koharski in the arena corridor. In front of several earwitnesses, Schoenfeld began his rant by saying the official was "full of shit". Some say he even pushed the referee. Schoenfeld went on to suggest that Koharski had a weight problem. "Have another donut, you fat pig," came spilling out of his mouth.

This from a guy who always looked so poised and unflappable when he was shilling for a mattress company on TV.

Schoenfeld acted surprised when his outburst earned him an immediate suspension. His team's owners were not only surprised but also angered by the quick decision to punish their coach. They rushed off to converse with a friendly judge, no doubt arguing that freedom of speech was an issue to consider. The judge agreed and served the league with a restraining order, which allowed Schoenfeld to coach in the very next game. It was mind-boggling— the first time in NHL history a member club had defied the league's decision to suspend a coach or player.

"The Devils cannot tolerate the injustice that has been done to Jim Schoenfeld," barked team president Lou Lamoriello.

Meanwhile, the game officials were following the story closely. Prior to game four, led by veteran referee Dave Newell, they voted on a wildcat strike. "If Schoenfeld coaches, we won't show up," was their ultimatum. And they didn't.

The incident was a disgrace to hockey, a shameful part of Stanley Cup history.

The game was delayed for an hour while a frantic search began for substitute officials. Oh, how the Jersey crowd hooted and howled when 52-year-old part-time referee Paul McInnis skated out with linesmen Vic Godleski, 51, and Jim Sullivan, 50. The linesmen looked ridiculous in their yellow practice jerseys, green pants, and borrowed skates. At least the referee had found a zebra shirt somewhere.

They looked very nervous, terribly uncomfortable.

Hockey Night in Canada's Don Cherry, an expert on sartorial trends, was not impressed. "They look gawdawful," he stated. "As for what Schoenfeld did, it was nothing. I've seen worse dozens of times. When I coached in Boston, Harry Sinden would kick in the door of the officials' dressing room to get at them."

Surprisingly, the game was played without incident. Perhaps the players on both teams decided to make things as easy as possible for the nervous fill-ins.

The Devils won the game 3–1 but lost the series four games to three. After the game four fiasco, Boston general manager Harry Sinden snorted, "The difference between those three old guys we pulled from the stands and our highly paid professionals was very marginal."

The three conscripted officials enjoyed an afternoon in hockey's lime-light. They got paid handsomely, and referee McInnis appeared on *Good Morning America* briefly the following morning, enjoying his 15 minutes of fame. Within days, their names were forgotten. Even the best of trivia buffs can't name the three substitute officials who worked the game that day.

The biggest surprise of the weekend's "donut dispute" came when NHL officials tried frantically—and unsuccessfully—to locate NHL president John Ziegler. They required his input and he had simply disappeared, gone like Jimmy Hoffa. When he surfaced a couple of days later, a red-faced Ziegler refused to divulge where he'd been. One insider leaked the rumour that he'd been playing golf with some friends somewhere in the Carolinas. Golf? On the day of a playoff game? If true, no wonder he wanted to keep it a secret.

The Bruins eliminated the Devils in the 1988 playoffs, but it didn't do them much good. They were swept aside in four straight games in the finals by the Edmonton Oilers.

Here's a postscript I was told by Don Koharski.

"On the Monday morning following the hectic weekend in New Jersey, my wife went shopping. She stepped into a Tim Hortons donut shop in Oakville, Ontario, where she was well known, and ordered a dozen to go. When she looked around, all the hockey fans in the place were laughing. For a moment, she wondered why. Then she got it and started laughing with them."

Kid from Hell's Kitchen Owns Three Stanley Cup Rings

When Joey Mullen was a kid, he had no ice to play on and no hockey sticks to play with. He didn't even own a pair of skates. Hockey was no big deal in the rough neighborhood where he grew up—in Hell's Kitchen, New York. He was almost in his teens before he learned to skate. Prior to that, all the hockey he enjoyed was played on asphalt and cement—roller hockey. But Joey—and his brother Brian—were lucky. Their father, Tom Mullen, had a job at Madison Square Garden. Occasionally, the Mullen boys got to skate on the Garden ice. They met most of the New York Rangers and collected broken and battered sticks from the NHL stars. They signed up to play in a minor league at another rink and dreamed of someday leading the Rangers to the Stanley Cup. Naive? You bet. Nobody gave them a chance in a million of ever fulfilling that dream.

But both Mullens chased their dream. They became skilled players, and both made it all the way to the NHL. But it wasn't easy, especially for older brother Joey. Branded as too small and too slow, the big-league scouts simply shrugged when his name was mentioned. Not bad, not great, was their assessment. Even after teenage Joey scored 110 goals in 40 games one season with an amateur team, the New York Westsiders, no eyebrows shot up, no agents came calling. Only after he recorded 32 and 34 goals in seasons with Boston College did hockey folks begin to pay attention.

Eventually, Joey signed on as a free agent with the St. Louis Blues and was shuffled off to play with their minor-league club in Salt Lake City. It was his chance to prove that all the scouts had been wrong about him, and he played far above anyone's expectations, scoring 40 goals one season, 59 the next. That opened some eyes. It wasn't long before he was a regular on the Blues' roster. He scored 25 goals in 45 games in 1981–82.

In a 16-year career spanning 1,062 games, Mullen scored 502 career goals in the NHL, the most by any U.S.–born player at the time he retired (his record has since been surpassed by Mike Modano). Mullen averaged a point a game with five different clubs. He played a key role on three Stanley Cup winners—not with the Rangers, his first love, but with Calgary in 1989 and Pittsburgh in 1991 and 1992. He also captured two Lady Byng Trophies as hockey's most gentlemanly player.

Not bad for a kid who was too small, too slow, and too late getting started in hockey to amount to anything.

In November, 2000, Mullen added another ring to his collection—this one signifying his induction into the Hockey Hall of Fame.

What about Brian Mullen, you ask? What happened to Joey's brother?

He too went from roller hockey and a job as the stickboy for visiting teams at Madison Square Garden to a college career at Wisconsin. He was signed by the Winnipeg Jets in 1982 and played on a line with star centreman Dale Hawerchuk for five seasons. He consistently scored between 20 and 30 goals per season. Between 1982 and 1992 he played with the Jets, the Rangers, the San Jose Sharks, and the New York Islanders. His biggest playoff thrill was helping the Islanders dethrone the two-time champion Pittsburgh Penguins in 1993. The series went seven games before the Islanders completed the upset with a win in overtime.

Two months later, he suffered a small stroke, caused by a hole in his heart through which a blood clot had moved upward, entering his brain. After open-heart surgery he was back on skates. But a year later in training camp, only minutes after learning the Islanders planned to send him to the minors, he suffered another seizure. Doctors told him his hockey career—which lasted 832 NHL games, during which he scored 260 goals and recorded 622 points—was over.

Winning the Cup Comes Easy for Some

Players like Bill Gadsby, who excelled in the NHL for 20 years without winning a Stanley Cup, will tell you: "It's so hard to win the damn thing. You've got to be in the right place at the right time. And even then, a hot goaltender or a couple of injuries to key players, and the Cup can slip away from you just when you think you've got it in your grasp. It can be very, very frustrating."

At least four former NHLers might reply: "Hey, Bill! What's the big deal? We won the Stanley Cup every year for the first five seasons we played in the league. And some of us won a few more after that."

It's true. Hall of Famer Henri Richard, along with teammates Jean-Guy Talbot, Claude Provost, and Bob Turner, played on the Montreal Canadiens during their dynasty years—1955–56 to 1959–60. Every spring, the Stanley Cup would be on display at the Montreal Forum. You could count on it.

Of the four Habs who began their careers with five in a row, Richard is the most famous. He was the darling of the Montreal fans for 20 seasons, almost as popular as his legendary brother, Rocket Richard.

"And just as hard to stop," Leaf defenceman Carl Brewer once told me.

Once labelled "too small to be a star," Henri Richard played in more games than any other Montreal player and has his name engraved on the Cup a record 11 times.

"I was lucky when it came to winning the Cup," Richard shrugs. "Right place at the right time."

Claude Provost played for 15 seasons, all with Montreal, and his name is on the Cup in nine places. Bob Turner, after his five consecutive Cup wins, played one more season with the Habs and three more with the Blackhawks. Jean-Guy Talbot won two more Cups with Montreal for a total of seven. He also played with Minnesota, Detroit, St. Louis, and Buffalo.

A large number of players have won four consecutive Stanley Cups. Several were members of the Canadiens from 1975–76 to 1978–79. Others played for the New York Islanders from 1979–80 to 1982–83. Several Edmonton Oilers were on five Cup winners in the '80s, but the wins were not consecutive.

Hall of Famer Red Kelly is the only non-Montreal player to hold eight Stanley Cup rings—four with Detroit and four more with Toronto.

Long before the formation of the NHL, members of the famed Ottawa Silver Seven won four consecutive Cups from 1902–03 to 1905–06. That era's most prolific scorer, "One-Eyed" Frank McGee, the only man to score 14 goals in a Stanley Cup game, was a member of this team. McGee scored almost three goals per game—63 in 22 Stanley Cup matches.

Leetch and Messier Bring the Cup to New York

When New York Rangers' defenceman Brian Leetch was voted MVP of the 1994 Stanley Cup playoffs, he became the first American, and the first Ranger, to have his name engraved on the Conn Smythe Trophy since its inception in 1965. Following the Rangers' victory over the Vancouver Canucks, Leetch even got to speak with President Bill Clinton.

But Leetch, had he not made hockey a career, might just as easily have captured the Cy Young Award in baseball. For in high school in Connecticut, he was a phenom on the mound. Luckily for the Rangers, who drafted him ninth overall in 1986, Leetch chose the ice over the diamond.

I recall sitting in Phil Esposito's office back in 1986. The Rangers' manager was talking about his team's number one draft choice. "You know Orr, eh? And Park? Well, we're going to get this kid Leetch and he's going to be like them. Well, maybe not like Orr. But he's going to take New York by storm. He's an American kid, born in Texas, of all places. And what an athlete! Hockey or baseball—great at both. Thank God he loves hockey more than baseball. I can't wait to get him here."

Almost two decades later, in 1994, Leetch was clutching the Conn Smythe Trophy and celebrating the Rangers' first Stanley Cup win since 1941. The Rangers, coached by Mike Keenan, had been thrown a scare by the

Vancouver Canucks, but had emerged with a 3–2 win in game seven to send Rangers' fans into a frenzy.

It was fitting that, after appearing on a dozen TV shows following the Rangers' Cup victory, Leetch should wind up at Yankee Stadium, accompanied by teammates Mark Messier and Nick Kypreos. The three Rangers took batting practice, but the Yankees neglected to ask Leetch to throw a few from the mound. Perhaps they weren't aware of it, but in high school, he had a fastball clocked at more than 90 miles per hour.

There was little doubt that Leetch would become one of the greatest U.S.–born hockey players ever. He played one year of college hockey at Boston College, where he was named to the All-America team, a rarity for a freshman player. He was also a finalist for the Hobey Baker Award, which goes to college hockey's top player—and he was the first freshman player to be nominated. He joined the Rangers for 17 games in 1988, following the Calgary Olympics, and in 1988–89 he won the Calder Trophy after setting a record for rookie defencemen with 23 goals. His 71-point total as a rookie is second only to Larry Murphy, who had 76 points in 1980–81.

The Rangers could not have won the Stanley Cup in '94 without him. He led all scorers with 11 goals and 23 assists for 34 points. The only defenceman to score more playoff points in a season is Paul Coffey, who amassed 37 with Edmonton in 1985. Leetch also became the first Ranger to lead all playoff scorers since Pentti Lund tallied 11 points in 12 games in 1950.

As great as Leetch was in '94, his teammate, Mark Messier, surpassed him in popularity with the Rangers' fans. Messier had vowed to bring the Stanley Cup to New York "or die trying," and his leadership was largely responsible for ending the baffling Ranger Cup curse that stretched back 54 years. The Rangers' captain had prodded his mates to do better all season, and the result was a franchise record 52 wins, 112 points and first place overall. Messier's dominance and charisma during the finals saw TV ratings for game seven on ESPN soar to 5.2—making it the most-watched broadcast of an NHL game in U.S. history.

Fittingly, Messier scored the Cup winner, the goal that ended The Curse.

New York City police anticipated a wild celebration following the Rangers' triumph, but Rangers' fans, while noisy and exuberant, were well behaved. They kept things under control. Strangely, Vancouver police were unable to do the same. Rioting broke out in the home of the Canucks and one man was critically injured. Over 20 criminal charges were laid, and as many as 200 people were hurt, including six officers.

On June 17, an estimated 1.5 million cheered the Rangers as they were paraded down the "Canyon of Heroes." But police were again able to keep things under control.

I was acting as MC at the Canadian Society of New York's annual hockey dinner that night. The 1,100 hockey fans in attendance shook the Waldorf-Astoria to its foundations with their victory roar and shouts of glee when Rangers' coach Mike Keenan made a stunning surprise entrance holding the Cup over his shoulders.

Not long after the New York Rangers won the 1994 Stanley Cup, general manager Neil Smith and coach Mike Keenan invited the players and their wives to a team function at the St. Regis Hotel in Manhattan. At the end of the meal, two dozen waiters entered the dining room carrying carved wooden boxes on trays. There were gasps from the men and women in the room when the boxes were opened. Inside each was a stunning memento of the Cup victory—a 10-karat diamond-studded gold ring. Then the Stanley Cup, on a pedestal in the room, was turned so that the players could see the 44 names freshly engraved on it. It was an emotional few moments. But there were two names missing—Ed Olczyk's and Mike Hartman's. Neither player had played in the required number of games (40) to be eligible to enjoy hockey's ultimate reward—having their names engraved on the Cup. The two veterans had come agonizingly close. Olczyk had played in 37 games, Hartman 35.

Both players knew there were strict rules about name engraving on the Cup, enforced after Peter Pocklington had placed his father's name on the trophy and engravers had to be called upon to cross it out with Xs. They sat there, lumps in their throats, until Neil Smith announced: "Both Mike

Gartner and I have protested the exclusion of the names Olczyk and Hartman from this trophy. Mike is president of the NHL Players' Association and an ex-Ranger [in fact, he had played 71 games for New York in 1993–94, before a trade-deadline deal sent him to Toronto]. Commissioner Gary Bettman asked us to be patient while he thought about the exclusions. Today, Mr. Bettman phoned me to say he would permit the names Olczyk and Hartman to be added to the Rangers' listing. Folks, the Stanley Cup will be going back to the engravers tomorrow."

Cheers filled the room as Olczyk and Hartman were rewarded with a standing ovation.

[Author's note: Perhaps Commissioner Bettman will consider doing something similar for Don Awrey of the Habs who was overlooked in 1973.]

Uwe Krupp: The First German Stanley Cup Hero

I met Uwe Krupp at the Montreal Forum one night and was amazed at his gargantuan size. He was a Buffalo rookie then—drafted 214th in 1983—and he was making his NHL debut against the Montreal Canadiens. He was from Germany—the only German-born NHLer at that time. At six feet, six inches and close to 250 pounds, he towered over everyone in the league. Would he last 15 seasons and become a Stanley Cup hero? The thought never occurred to me.

By the spring of 1996, Krupp had travelled from the Buffalo Sabres to the New York Islanders to the Quebec Nordiques. The Nordiques fled Quebec to settle in Colorado in 1995-96. Renamed the Avalanche, in the spring of '96, the Avs became the first team in NHL history to win a Stanley Cup while playing their first season in a new city. The Avs swept the Florida Panthers aside in four games in the finals. They were never in trouble, outscoring the Panthers 15-4. Joe Sakic led all playoff scorers with 18 goals and 34 points and was a popular winner of the Conn Smythe Trophy as playoff MVP.

But the unlikely hero in the deciding game was the German giant, Uwe Krupp. Krupp scored the game's only goal—the series winner—at 4:31 of the third overtime period. Krupp became the first German-born player to win a Stanley Cup, the first German-born NHL All-Star, and the first to have a lasting and impressive NHL career. His heroics that spring may have been overshadowed by a black mark cast on the game by the Avs' Claude Lemieux, who laid a vicious check on Detroit's Kris Draper in the Western Conference finals. Draper wound up with a fractured jaw and cheekbone, a broken nose, a cut inside his mouth requiring 30 stitches, and five teeth that required re-alignment.

"I didn't even have a chance to protect myself," Draper said bitterly. "But that's the kind of player Lemieux is. Everybody knows it."

Red Wing goalie Chris Osgood said angrily, "It's the last time Lemieux is going to get away with something like that. He's got four months to get ready for next season. It's no secret what we're going to try and do to him."

Lemieux received a major penalty and a game misconduct penalty on the play. "I didn't think it was too bad, maybe deserving of two minutes," he said.

When the next season rolled around, what did the Red Wings do to Lemieux to pay him back?

Nothing.

Krupp played for Detroit and Florida in the twilight of his career. Then shoulder, back, and knee surgery forced him to retire.

Back in Germany, shortly before the Olympic Games in Torino, Italy, Krupp was appointed coach of Germany's national team. Boldly, he cast aside seven veterans of the team, including the leading scorer, and selected a team of youngsters—average age 22. The German media roasted him. But his young club sailed past Israel, Hungary, Great Britain, Japan and France, outscoring opponents 35-4 as they ascended into the "A" group of the Olympics.

Well done, Uwe!

Worth noting: The Avs should have sent thank-you notes to both Eric Lindros and Mario Tremblay following their Stanley Cup victory. Because Lindros refused to report to Quebec when they drafted him, he was traded to Philadelphia. Two ex-Flyers, Peter Forsberg and Mike Ricci, performed superbly for the Avs, as did goalie Patrick Roy. Roy, one of hockey's premier goaltenders, was dealt to the Avs following a flare-up when he played with Montreal for coach Mario Tremblay. Tremblay had let Roy suffer through a humiliating loss to Detroit and Roy's pride was stung. Furious, he stormed up to club president Ron Corey and announced, "I'll never play for this team again." A few days later, he was traded to the Avalanche. Before the season was over, he had helped his new team to the Stanley Cup.

Wings End 42-Year Drought

In the spring of 1997, the Detroit Red Wings began a final charge for the Stanley Cup against the Philadelphia Flyers. Even though they were bolstered by newfound confidence, the Wings had difficulty putting past failures from their minds. Sour thoughts of their four-game loss to the Devils two years earlier, and the bitter recollection of their six-game defeat to Colorado in 1996, were hard to dispel—not to mention constant reminders that it had been 42 years since a Red Wings' team had sipped bubbly from the trophy.

That's why it was a major surprise when the Wings swept the bigger, supposedly tougher Flyers aside in four straight games—the third time in a row the final series ended in a rout. Long shot goals killed the Flyers in games one and two—the first against Ron Hextall, the second against Garth Snow. It was smart thinking for Scotty Bowman to have his snipers shoot from centre ice. It guaranteed there'd be no review from the video judge's booth. An annoying number of video replays of in-the-crease goals had marred the entire playoffs.

After the Wings captured game three on home ice, Flyer coach Terry Murray said his team was in a "choking situation," words that infuriated his GM Bob Clarke. But they didn't ignite a torch under the team, for the Wings skated off with a 2–1 victory in game four. His mates immediately mobbed goalie Mike Vernon. Moments later, Vernon held high the Conn Smythe

Trophy as the playoff MVP. He had not only backstopped Detroit to the elusive Stanley Cup, winning 16 games after winning just 13 in the regular season, but he earned himself a handsome $200,000 bonus for capturing the MVP award plus an automatic $2.3 million (U.S.) contract extension.

A few weeks after the Wings triumphed, there was a touching scene at an arena in the Ottawa suburb of Nepean.

In late August, Steve Yzerman brought the Stanley Cup to the town where he played his minor hockey and where he once led a pee wee team to the provincial championship.

Yzerman carefully removed the Cup from the back of his white convertible and walked along the red carpet that brought him before a couple of thousand people gathered in the new Steve Yzerman Arena.

In the crowd that day was another Steve—an old friend named Steve Unger. As a teenager, Unger shared Yzerman's love for hockey, and he played the game with the same skill and enthusiasm. Like Yzerman, he had played for the Nepean Raiders. He was a centreman who hoped someday to be a star in the NHL. Everybody said his chances were good.

But in 1984, the 16-year-old suffered a broken neck when he dove into the waters of Brittania Bay. He was left paralyzed, a quadriplegic.

Following the accident, Yzerman and former Nepean goalie Darren Pang approached several friends and acquaintances, raised some money, and set up a trust fund for their crippled pal. Before long, Unger had a new van he could drive himself. He had a dog by his side—one who could even bring him drinks from the fridge. Unger will be forever grateful for the generosity and the compassion shown by those around him, especially old friends and teammates who pitched in to help.

Suddenly, Yzerman spotted Unger in the crowd and, without hesitating, walked over to the smiling man in the wheelchair. Gently, the NHL star placed the gleaming trophy in Unger's lap. Tears welled up in Unger's eyes as the crowd filled the arena with their cheers and applause. Steve Yzerman, hockey superstar, and Steve Unger, who might have been one, shared a very precious moment.

I interviewed 19-year-old Steve Yzerman on *Hockey Night in Canada* in 1984 at his first All-Star game, and I remember how impressed I was with the manner in which he conducted himself. It wasn't long before he was named Detroit's captain, a role he would assume for the next 20 years—a league record.

Before Yzerman's arrival, season-ticket sales for Red Wings' games were abysmal. The club was called the Dead Wings. When he blossomed, season-ticket sales tripled and quadrupled.

Konstantinov Almost Dies in Post-Season Disaster

Hanging over the 1997 Stanley Cup post-season victory celebrations in Detroit, a few short days following the Red Wings' ouster of the Philadelphia Flyers, were thoughts and prayers for the Wings' star defenceman Vladimir Konstantinov, who was in a coma in hospital after a car accident that left him critically injured.

Konstantinov grew up in the town of Murmansk, north of the Arctic Circle. He was one of the best teenage hockey stars in that cold, remote, and frigid place, an aggressive young defenceman who was recruited by the famous Red Army team in Moscow in 1984 when he was only 17. By 1989, after five years (and four World Championships) he was named Red Army's captain.

Throughout the 1990–91 season, he yearned to join countryman Sergei Fedorov in Detroit. Fedorov had defected from the Russian team during the Goodwill Games in Seattle in 1990, but Konstantinov, drafted 221st overall in 1989, would have to find another route to the NHL.

Following the dispersal of a large amount of bribe money, certain Russian officials confirmed a medical diagnosis that Konstantinov had a rare form of cancer, a type that could only be treated in the United States. After papers were signed and stamped, he was allowed to leave Moscow. He made the long trip to Detroit and never looked back. And he was never treated for cancer.

In the NHL, he soon gained a reputation as one of the game's most feared defencemen, dishing out devastating body checks and using his stick on anyone who challenged him. In the media, he was called Vlad the Impaler and Bad Vlad.

But Detroit fans loved him. He was named to the All-Rookie team after the 1991–92 season, and in 1995–96 he led all NHL players in plus-minus with a fabulous rating of plus-60.

The sweetest of all his six NHL seasons was 1996–97, when he helped lead the Red Wings to the coveted Stanley Cup. In the finals, the Wings swept Philadelphia aside in four straight games. Lord Stanley's old basin hadn't been seen in Hockeytown since 1955.

After sweeping the Flyers, the Red Wings were saluted by a million fans who turned out for a downtown rally in their honour. Konstantinov, a candidate for the Norris Trophy as the league's best defenceman (he would finish behind the Rangers' Brian Leetch), held the Cup aloft. "This Cup is for you, for Detroit, for Michigan," he shouted.

The players attended a final team function before dispersing for the summer. It was a golf outing on June 13, followed by a team party at the home of goalie Chris Osgood.

Limousines took the players from the golf course to the Osgood residence. Konstantinov, Sergei Fetisov, and team masseur Sergei Mnatsakanov hopped into a limo driven by Richard Gnida, whose drivers' licence, it was later revealed, had been revoked following several violations. He was driving through Birmingham, Michigan, when the huge vehicle careened out of control, smashing into a tree.

A police report stated that the limo's brakes had not been applied, and that Gnida was found to have marijuana in his system. Possibly he fell asleep at the wheel.

His three passengers barely survived. Fetisov suffered a leg injury, but Konstantinov and Mnatsakanov struck the partition in the limo headfirst. They were rushed to hospital, suffering from severe brain trauma and other injuries.

The horrific accident ended any further Stanley Cup celebrations. Teammate Igor Larionov, a daily visitor to the hospital, said, "You see Vlad holding the Stanley Cup, so happy, so proud, so strong. And now he's in a coma. He's lost 30 pounds. It's very sad, very emotional."

In midsummer, Konstantinov and Mnatsakanov began to emerge from their comas. A neurosurgeon said, "We're encouraged, but it's too early to say anything about a full recovery."

Teammates brought the gleaming Stanley Cup into the hospital, and Konstantinov's hand was placed on its surface. No one knows if he recognized it; no one knows what he felt. His Russian teammates had planned to bring the Cup to Moscow in August. Now they would have to go without him. It would have been his first time back home.

On November 7, 1997, Richard Gnida, the limousine driver, was sentenced to nine months in jail and 15 months on probation. He was also ordered to attend Alcoholics Anonymous meetings four times a week and get counselling. "You shattered lives," Judge Kimberly Small told Gnida.

On the following day, Konstantinov was able to attend a ceremony at which the Red Wings received their Stanley Cup rings. Sitting in his wheelchair, he held his ring and brushed aside tears as his teammates surrounded him, patting him on the back and shaking him gently by the hand.

When the Stanley Cup champs were honoured at the White House in January, 1998, President Bill Clinton said he was "thrilled" to be able to meet Konstantinov, whom he called a player with "the heart of a champion." Clinton posed for a photo with the great Russian player, who had been moved to a private rehabilitation clinic in Florida. The president said the photo would heighten his popularity in Russia. "Vlad, we know how hard you've been working and how far you've come," he told the indestructible Red Wing. Konstantinov nodded his head, indicating he understood the message. He received a standing ovation from all those assembled.

Team captain Steve Yzerman, after presenting the president with a Detroit jersey emblazoned with the name Clinton and the number one on the back, pointed out that the last time the Red Wings held the Stanley Cup was in 1955, when Dwight D. Eisenhower was president. "But I don't think Ike was much of a hockey fan," quipped Yzerman. "So Gordie and the boys never got an invite to the White House."

When coach Scotty Bowman presented the president with a replica of the Stanley Cup, Mr. Clinton told him, "Scotty, you've won this trophy so many times they should call it the Stanley Bowman Cup."

The Red Wings won the Cup again that season, ousting Washington in the finals in four straight games.

And they captured it for a third time in 2001–02, defeating the Carolina Hurricanes in a five-game series. Three Cups in six years doesn't quite qualify them as a dynasty. But it brought great satisfaction to owner Mike Ilitch and his family. Ilitch bought the struggling Red Wing franchise in 1982 for $8 million. Ten years later, it was valued at over $200 million.

Brett Hull's Tainted Goal Brings Cup to Texas

During the 1998–99 NHL season, the game officials stopped play more than 200 times to seek video help in ruling on goal-crease violations. If it looked as though the toe of a player's skate was on or over the edge of the crease, time-outs were called until the legality of the invasion could be determined.

Incredibly, on the one occasion when officials should have sought help and called for a review of a possible winning goal for the Stanley Cup—the most important goal of the year—they neglected to do so and the season was over. The Dallas Stars were dancing around the ice holding the Stanley Cup while the Buffalo Sabres were crushed.

Writing in *The Hockey News*, then editor-in-chief Steve Dryden called it "a mystifying conclusion" and added, "The NHL left pieces of their credibility on the ice."

Game six of the Stanley Cup finals between Buffalo and Dallas was in triple overtime when the Stars' Brett Hull shovelled the biggest goal of his career past Dominik Hasek, ending the second-longest Cup final game in NHL history.

But should it have ended? Buffalo fans have been screaming, "We were robbed!" ever since. Hull's foot was clearly in the crease when he slipped in the winning goal. But NHL director of officiating Bryan Lewis and his colleagues looked at the goal and allowed it to stand.

Lewis said: "The debate seems to be: did Hull have or not have possession and control of the puck? Our view was yes, he did. He played the puck from his foot to his stick, then shot and scored."

Buffalo coach Lindy Ruff, and millions of others, didn't buy it. Ruff was outraged by the swiftness of the decision. He could not understand why there was no official video review of the series-ending goal. "I tried to get Commissioner Gary Bettman to answer the question, and he just turned his back on me. It looked to me like he knew this was a tainted goal. I just wanted an explanation," said Ruff.

Buffalo fans were baffled and bitter. They howled that Hull's goal was tarnished and they demanded proof that it wasn't. But they didn't get it.

"What a gutless move!" snarled Buffalo's Joe Juneau. "Everybody will remember this one as the Cup that was never won in 1999."

As for Hull the hero, he shouldn't even have been on the ice. Nursing a torn ligament in his left knee, a groin muscle ripped apart, and other aches and pains, he was told his season was over after game three of the series. But he refused to believe it.

So there he was, limping through the second-longest final game ever played, until he ran out of gas. "Hull is done. He can't go anymore," assistant coach Doug Jarvis told head coach Ken Hitchcock. Hitchcock agreed and replied, "I won't play him anymore."

But two other Stars went down and the coach was forced to send Hull out for one last shift. He limped toward the Buffalo net, got his stick on a loose puck, and lifted it in.

The Dallas players leaped off the bench and mobbed him. They were allowed to swarm and celebrate. There was no public announcement that the goal was under review, as is always the case. Confusion reigned. Grudgingly, the Sabres lined up to shake hands with the victors, even while the victory was in doubt.

"I couldn't have played a game seven," Hull would say.

"No one knows how much grit it took for him to be out there," marvelled coach Hitchcock. "What an incredible job our trainers did to make it possible. He was a modern-day Bobby Baun."

Rosie DiManno, writing in the *Toronto Star*, stated: "The gallant Buffalo Sabres will go to their graves believing they were robbed and jobbed by that 2–1 defeat at 14:51 of triple overtime. Who can blame them?

"Coach Lindy Ruff should have brought all his players back to the bench, there to await an official announcement [of the goal's legality], to force one from the officials. He should not have allowed his players to participate in the hand-shaking ritual that declares the series over. But that's hindsight. In a league that has no foresight. A league blinded by its own incompetence."

During the season—and on into the playoffs—crease rule violations were so rampant that the league had already decided to adopt a "no harm, no foul" rule for the following season.

Hull's controversial goal overshadowed teammate Joe Nieuwendyk's six game-winning goals in the playoffs, which tied a playoff record and earned him the Conn Smythe Trophy.

And it far overshadowed a goal by another teammate, Craig Ludwig. In game two, Ludwig scored his first playoff goal in 11 years, the longest time between goals by any player.

Brett Hull would taste Stanley Cup Champagne once more—in 2002, after joining the Detroit Red Wings. He retired in 2005 following a brief stint with Phoenix. Hull is third on the all time goal-scoring list with 741, behind Wayne Gretzky and Gordie Howe and ahead of his father, who is twelfth on the list with 640 career goals. There has never been a father-son combination as prolific as the Hulls.

Throw Dennis Hull into the mix with his 303 career goals and you've the best father-son-uncle combination in the business.

"Too bad my sister Maxine didn't get to play in the NHL," Dennis says with a wink. "Maxine could outscore any of us."

Andreychuk Bows Out a Winner

Hall of Fame defenceman Bill Gadsby played in the NHL for 20 seasons and never sipped from a Stanley Cup.

In 2003–04, forward Dave Andreychuk, winding down an impressive career with Tampa Bay, figured he was likely to feel the same sense of disappointment Gadsby knew so well. Andreychuk was about to conclude his 22nd season in the NHL without a Cup to show for all those years.

After the final regular-season game, when a reporter reminded the Tampa Bay captain he had played in more games than any other player never to have won a Stanley Cup, Andreychuk replied, "It's not too late. We're in the playoffs, aren't we?"

Indeed, Tampa Bay was in the playoffs. The team that had finished 29th in the standings two seasons earlier had fought its way to the top of its division, with 106 points, only three fewer than first-place Detroit. Swift little Martin St. Louis, the ex–college player from Vermont, had provided much of the spark, winning the scoring title with 94 points.

Then Brad Richards put together one of the all-time clutch performances in playoff history, popping in seven game-winning goals, while goalie Nikolai Khabibulin posted a 16–7 record in the postseason, with five shutouts and a 1.71 goals-against average.

"It was awesome," Andreychuk said. "We kept coming up with big games and suddenly we're facing Calgary for the Cup. I would have one more chance at it—my last chance."

The series went seven games, with the deciding game played on Tampa Bay ice on June 7. Early in the game, another Lightning hero emerged. Ruslan Fedotenko, a native of Kiev in the Ukraine, scored twice. The Flames got one puck past Khabibulin, but that was all. The Lightning won by a 2–1 score and captain Andreychuk finally was able to kiss the Cup and hold it high.

"This is more than I ever expected," he said, his face aglow. "As a kid I dreamed of a moment like this. I just never thought it would happen. Not at age 40."

After the celebration on the ice, Brad Richards was awarded the Conn Smythe Trophy as playoff MVP. "Winning the Cup was our main focus," he said. "Holding the Smythe Trophy is a real bonus—and a great honour."

A few days later, at the annual NHL Awards dinner, Richards would be awarded the Lady Byng Trophy for sportsmanship, while St. Louis was reeling in the Art Ross Trophy (leading scorer), the Hart Trophy (league MVP), and the Pearson Award (players' choice for MVP).

Lightning coach John Tortorella, awarded the Jack Adams Trophy as coach of the year, was almost at a loss for words. Almost, but not quite.

"I can't believe our team got here so fast," he said. "Winning the Cup was totally unexpected. It wasn't in our plan. Well, it was, but not quite so soon."

The Tampa Bay victory was followed by a year-long lockout of the players. The lockout gave the league time to plot out new rules designed to eliminate hooking and holding and speed up the game.

Andreychuk, never fleet of foot, but fast enough to cash in 640 career goals for 11th place on the all-time goal-scoring list, decided to retire midway through the 2005–06 season—his 23rd in the NHL.

A postscript: Tampa Bay defenceman Pavel Kubina spent an emotional three days with the Cup. He took it to his home in the Czech Republic, to the small town of Janovice.

"My town has a population of about 2,000. But when I held a big party for the Cup on a soccer field there, about 8,000 people showed up. There was so much excitement and so much traffic you couldn't move. Then I took the Cup to the president of the Czech Republic. His name is Václav Klaus. He was very interested and spent almost an hour with me. I even gave him a Tampa Bay jersey with his name on the back."

Dominik Hasek: Next Stop, Hall of Fame

When he skated away from a contract in 2002, one that would have paid him $8 million for one more season in Detroit, goaltender Dominik Hasek had no regrets.

"My decision to retire at age 37 was never about money," he explained. "After 21 years of playing the game at the highest level, I felt I didn't have the same fire to compete at that level anymore."

The Red Wings pleaded with him to stay. So did over a million fans who cheered him during the Red Wings' Stanley Cup parade, two days after his team's 2002 victory over the Carolina Hurricanes in the finals. He left with the lowest career goals-against average (2.23) of any of the retired goalies of hockey's modern era and a record of six shutouts in the 2002 post-season.

But the "Dominator" could not be swayed. He had achieved his ultimate goal in hockey—a Stanley Cup—and he'd had enough. "It was an easy decision," he explained. "How many players get to go out on top?"

Next stop for Hasek and his family: a return to the Czech Republic where he'd been a hockey legend for more than a decade and where he began his working life as a high school history teacher.

He had compiled an incredible record of accomplishment. Aside from his Stanley Cup, there were Olympic gold and bronze medals, six Vezina

Trophies, two Hart Trophies, two Pearson Awards, two Jennings Awards, six First All-Star Team selections, and a berth on the All-Rookie Team. Not a bad career for a goalie who was traded by Chicago in 1992 for a netminder they prized more highly—Stephane Beauregard—plus a draft choice who turned out to be Eric Daze. Beauregard? Lasted 90 games, winning only 19.

But Hasek's "easy decision to retire" didn't last more than a year. The itch to play was still there. He returned to Detroit for the 2003–04 season, but injured his groin after just 14 games and was lost for the season. He told the Wings he felt uncomfortable about being paid when he could not play and settled for half of his $6 million salary.

A year later, he turned up in Ottawa, signing a one-year contract, and was hopeful of leading a powerful team to the Stanley Cup. Again he injured his groin and missed the rest of the season. Without him, Ottawa missed the Cup.

Undaunted, at age 41, the second-oldest player in the NHL (next to the Wings' Chris Chelios, who is still playing at age 46), he returned once again to Detroit for the 2006–07 season—at a salary of $750,000.

And he decided to stay around for the 2007–08 season. He was rewarded with another championship, although he was used only sparingly during the Red Wings' playoff run. On June 9, 2008, five days after he hoisted the Cup with his mates, Hasek announced his retirement. This time, it seemed he was quitting for good—but with the Dominator, one never knows.

There may be only one major hockey honour left for the Dominator: induction into the Hockey Hall of Fame. And that could be the most meaningful moment of them all for the man who, in the past, was often referred to as "the greatest goalie on the planet."

Bordering on the Bizarre

The Stanley Cup playoffs bring out the best and the worst in people. When emotions run high, anything can happen. Stories of love, hate, anger, and fear abound. And many of the bizarre stories become, well, collector's items. Here are just a few.

Get Your Butt on the Ice

During the 1989 Stanley Cup playoffs, a Los Angeles disc jockey came up with a novel way to bring good luck to the L.A. Kings in their playoff battles. Before each game, with the sanction of Kings' owner Bruce McNall (before he served a prison term), the DJ dropped his drawers at centre ice and rubbed his naked butt over the faceoff circle at the Great Western Forum.

McNall laid down only one condition: the ritual must take place long before the paying customers arrived at the arena.

"I've never been a shy guy," the DJ said. "Even on my radio show, I've been told I show a lot of cheek. But never as much as I show before the Kings' games."

A Hungry Hockey Player

During a 1981 playoff battle between the Quebec Nordiques and the Philadelphia Flyers, Nordiques' goaltender Dan Bouchard, a gentle man—

indeed, a born-again Christian who believed in the Golden Rule—found himself in a wrestling match with diminutive but scrappy Ken Linseman of the Flyers.

Linseman had no compunction about breaking a few rules, written or otherwise.

When Bouchard tried to disengage himself from Linseman's grasp, he felt a sharp pain. "The so-and-so bit me on the hand," Bouchard said angrily. "Now I know where he got his nickname—Rat."

Oops! My Mistake

During the first game of the 1952 final series between Detroit and Montreal, the Red Wings held a 2–1 lead late in the third period. When Montreal coach Dick Irvin heard the public address announcer proclaim, "Last minute of play," he yanked his goalie and threw out an extra attacker. Ted Lindsay of the Wings promptly scored into the empty Montreal net. To Irvin's chagrin, the announcer then confessed he'd made a mistake— that he had announced the "last minute of play" a minute too early. Irvin wanted to throttle the man, blaming him for the empty-net goal and the possible tying goal. Detroit won 3–1 and went on to sweep the Habs in four games.

Do These Names Belong on the Cup?

When the Edmonton Oilers won the Stanley Cup in 1984, team owner Peter Pocklington thought it would be a neat idea to have his father's name engraved on the trophy. The NHL moguls were not amused and the name, while not erased, was covered over by a number of Xs. Pocklington, Sr.'s name came out XXXXXXX.

The Detroit Red Wings had injured player Vladimir Konstantinov's name engraved on the Cup in 1998, even though the Russian star, who suffered a brain injury in a post-season accident in 1997, did not play for the Red Wings that season.

Who is G. Bettex? That name appeared on the Cup after the Montreal Canadiens' victory in 1956. Bettex certainly wasn't a player. Was he a trainer, an equipment man, somebody's relative? Nobody seemed to know. Hall of Fame broadcaster Dick Irvin finally solved the mystery. "If the name Bettex is still on the Cup, it's a misspelling," he said. "Gaston Bettez was an obscure little assistant trainer for the Habs back when my father coached the club."

Demers No Penny-Pincher

Perhaps it was a sly trick by St. Louis Blues coach Jacques Demers that helped his team defeat the Minnesota North Stars in a best-of-five playoff series in 1986. During the series, when his team ran out of legal timeouts, Demers was caught furtively tossing pennies on the ice during stoppages in play. When asked to explain, Demers admitted he threw the coins around to give his players a few extra moments to catch their breath.

Demers replied, "No comment" when asked if he had learned the penny-tossing trick from coach Mike Keenan, then with Philadelphia. When Keenan was interrogated, he laughed and said, "I don't make that much money that I can afford to throw it around like Jacques. He's the highest-paid coach in the NHL."

Rooney Ties the Knot, Then Ties His Skates

In 1984, when Habs' forward Steve Rooney and his fiancée planned their wedding for an April day one year later, they never imagined Montreal and Boston would be meeting in a playoff game at the Boston Garden. But that's exactly what happened. And Rooney, a Montreal rookie, had to figure out how to be in two places at the same time. But you've probably guessed how he solved the problem. The wedding was moved to the morning. He tied the knot, kissed the bride, said "See you later", and rushed to the Garden, where his Canadiens eliminated the Bruins in the deciding game of their playoff series. Rooney even scored a goal.

From time to time, married couples reflect on their wedding day. They even ask each other what cherished memories they have of the event. If Rooney is smart, he won't say, "Gosh, honey, it has to be beating the Bruins and scoring that big goal."

Druce Produced

Forward John Druce, a right winger from Peterborough, Ontario, scored only eight goals for the Washington Capitals during the 1989–90 season. But he came through like Wayne Gretzky once the playoffs rolled around. In six games against New Jersey, he scored three times, and two of them were game winners. In the following series against the Rangers, Druce scored nine more goals and led his team into the conference finals against Boston.

The Bruins held the Caps to just six goals in their four-game sweep of Washington, but Druce's amazing scoring touch was the topic of every hockey conversation. He'd added two more goals, giving him 14 in 15 playoff games. He'd never enjoyed a scoring streak like it before, and never produced such numbers again. In fact, he performed in another 37 playoff games over the next few seasons and managed a mere three goals for a career total of 17.

A Foggy Day

When the Buffalo Sabres defeated the Philadelphia Flyers in the third game of the 1975 finals, our NBC team was there to cover the action. Problem was, we couldn't *see* the action. Fog hung over the ice of the arena, which had no air conditioning. It was so thick that Flyers goalie Bernie Parent quipped, "I wouldn't take my boat out in these conditions." Parent was beaten five times by "pucks I couldn't see. Next game I'll put windshield washers on my mask." His coach, Fred Shero, didn't think the conditions were funny. "Someone could have been killed out there. Collisions were inevitable."

The Flyers won the series in six games. Parent was named the most valuable player in the playoffs.

Orlando Arrested During 1943 Playoffs

Detroit tough guy Jimmy Orlando was arrested by the FBI in the middle of the 1943 playoffs and charged with draft evasion. He was accused of falsifying documents that stated he held an essential war job and was therefore exempt from military service. Orlando was convicted, but he avoided jail time by enlisting in the Canadian army.

Pre-Game Brawl Stuns Montreal Fans

In 1987, the Montreal Canadiens faced the Philadelphia Flyers in the Wales Conference finals. Prior to game six at the Montreal Forum, an astonishing incident took place. The Habs, at the end of their pre-game warmup, had begun a ritual of shooting the puck into the opposing team's empty net. On this night, the Habs' Claude Lemieux and Shayne Corson slipped back onto the ice to team up for the empty-net shot when Flyer goalie Chico Resch and tough guy Ed Hospodar raced from their dressing room to intercept the Montreal duo. Resch threw his stick at the puck, while Hospodar tried to hook Corson. Then Hospodar attacked Lemieux and pummelled him with his fists. Within seconds, both teams were back on the ice, some without their skates, and a bitter battle ensued.

Hospodar was suspended for the balance of the playoffs, and players from both teams were assessed fines totaling $24,500.

Canes Win Despite Koivu's Courage

Not all of my favourite Stanley Cup stories are about winners and champions. Sometimes a losing effort is just as memorable as a victory celebration.

Their Stanley Cup hopes crushed, the Montreal Canadiens skated though the final few seconds of game six of their 2002 playoff series against the Carolina Hurricanes on the wrong end of an 8–2 score.

Game over and season over.

But were Hab fans despondent? Did they jeer the players on the ice after such a humiliating defeat?

No, they roared themselves hoarse showing their approval of a gallant team and heroic players who had eliminated a tough Boston club only to lose to a tougher Carolina team.

They roared throughout the final seconds and long afterward for Saku Koivu, the little captain who had come back from a near-death experience, showing courage beyond belief.

No one expected to see the gutsy little guy out there. Not in the playoffs. It was too much and much too soon. Eight months earlier, Koivu had received terrible news. He was stricken with abdominal cancer. Some said he was finished with hockey, that his days were numbered, that he'd be fortunate to survive the invasion of this malicious disease.

But he fooled them all and came back to play as he'd always played, leading the Habs farther into the playoffs than anyone thought possible. His quick recovery bordered on the miraculous.

Now, in the final game, the seconds ticked away and then it was over.

And that's why they cheered and cheered and continued to cheer. It was the kind of tribute former Montreal idols—Beliveau, Richard, Lafleur—might have heard. But this ovation was different. It was one filled with love and respect and admiration for a 27-year-old Finn, his gaunt face covered with playoff stubble. They weren't saluting his goals and assists, although there were enough of those (4–6–10). They were hailing Captain Koivu—Captain "Courageous" Koivu.

Not all the cheers, mind you. He shared the prolonged ovation with another little guy—goaltender Jose Theodore. Without Theodore, there would have been no playoff action for the Habs.

"MVP, MVP!" shouted the fans, signifying their support for Theodore as the league's best player.

Theodore had been pulled from the final game when a comeback became unthinkable, an impossibility. But with 1:39 to play, coach Michel Therrien gave his goaltender a nod and Theodore skated back out. He played the final minute and a half while the crowd stood and applauded and shook the walls with their cheering.

"I was very moved by it," Theodore would say in the dressing room.

So was the little captain—Saku Koivu.

Several months later, in the old-timers' dressing room, we're into hockey trivia and someone throws out a tough question.

"Can you name the three rookie goaltenders who've led their teams to a Stanley Cup?" he asks.

"I can name one," Joe the goalie shouts across the room. "Ken Dryden. Back in '71. Montreal upset Boston, then beat Chicago in the finals." Then, with a straight face, Joe adds, "Did you guys know that

Dryden idolized me when he was a kid?"

We laugh. "Sure he did, Joe. Just like you idolized Georges Vezina. Anyway, that's one. How about two more?" our quizmaster asks.

"Is it Patrick Roy?" someone chirps. "I think he won the Cup as a rookie."

"You've got it. With Montreal in 1986. Now name me one more. One more name, guys. C'mon."

I stay out of it. I'm supposed to know the answers.

There's a long silence. Finally, Harry, one of the real old guys, so deaf it's a wonder he heard the question, jumps up, still in his long johns, waving his hand.

"I know. I know," he bellows. "Ron Hextall of the Flyers. Against Gretzky and the Oilers."

"You dummy. Hextall was the *losing* goalie against the Oilers."

"Oh, yeah, that's right. Wait! I think I've got it. The kid from Carolina. Cam... something. Cam Ward. A couple of years ago. He was a rookie, wasn't he?"

"Let's hear it for Harry!" shouts our questioner, and we all applaud. "Cam Ward it is. Someday all you dummies will be watching Harry on TV— on *Jeopardy!*"

I think of Cam Ward. And how little most of us know about him.

Howie Menard, a former pro sitting next to me, nudges me. "Ward's the kid from Sherwood Park near Edmonton, right? Carolina's number one draft choice in 2002, right?"

"Yep. The rookie led the Hurricanes to the Stanley Cup in 2006. And he did it by coming off the bench. It's a good story, a Cinderella story—although Cinderella would look funny trying to slip on one of Cam Ward's goal skates. I looked Ward up on the Internet the other day. I printed it off. There's some interesting stuff about him there."

"Like what?" asked Howie, bending over to pull on a skate.

"Like in the first round of the 2006 playoffs, when the Hurricanes' number one goalie, Martin Gerber, was a little shaky. His team fell two games behind the Montreal Canadiens. That's when Gerber was replaced by this kid

Ward, who carried the Hurricanes to the next round against New Jersey. Ward stayed hot and helped oust the Devils and his personal hero, Martin Brodeur.

"Then came Buffalo, as the Hurricanes inched closer to the Stanley Cup finals. The series went seven games and Ward was unflappable. Out went the Sabres.

"The kid never flinched under the pressure of the finals, either. The constant media attention didn't seem to bother him. He became the first rookie goalie in two decades to start a game in the finals, the first in two decades to record a shutout—a 5–0 win in game two. He tied the rookie record for wins in the playoffs with 15, and he became the first rookie goaltender to win the Conn Smythe Trophy since the Flyers' Ron Hextall captured it in 1987."

Howie was still looking down, working at his laces. He hadn't noticed me take a folded paper from my pocket.

"Geez," he said, struggling to thread a lace through an eyelet, "how do you remember all this stuff? What else do you know about this kid Ward?"

"Not much. He carried the Hurricanes through seven tense games against the Edmonton Oilers, giving up just 16 goals along the way. One of the goals was on a penalty shot scored by Chris Pronger. It was the first successful penalty shot in the history of the finals. Ward's solid goaltending cemented a 3–1 win, he wins the Cup, and the celebration begins."

Howie grunts. He still hasn't glanced up, hasn't seen the printout I've got in my hand.

"So the rookie wins the Cup," he says. "Good for him. End of story."

"Oh, he was happy," I say. "Even happier a few weeks later when he married his childhood sweetheart, Cody Campbell."

Howie chuckled.

"McFarlane," he says, "you must have a photographic memory to know all this crap."

"No, I'm just a trivia buff, Howie." I sneak a final look at the printout. "By the way, Ward is the second child of Ken and Laurel Ward. He has two sisters, Kendra and Chelsea. His nickname is Wardo and he likes watching the Saskatchewan Roughriders."

With that, I fold the paper I've been reading from and slip it back in my pocket.

Howie straightens up, turns, and grabs my hand. He looks at me admiringly. "I can't believe you have all that trivia in your head," he said.

Driving home after our game, I thought back to the old-timers' dressing room and the trivia question. Howie and the boys had successfully named three rookie goaltenders who'd won the Stanley Cup—Dryden, Roy, and Ward. Suddenly, I realized there was a fourth. It happened back in the '40s, just after the war, long before most of us began to follow hockey.

In the 1945 finals, rookie goalie Frank McCool of the Leafs, winner of the Calder Trophy that season, shut out Detroit in the first three games—an astonishing finals debut. But Detroit fought back and forced the series to the limit, only to have young McCool edge them 2–1 in the seventh game.

Was McCool unflappable, the way Ward is purported to be? No. He suffered from ulcers. If there'd been a goalie's bottle on the net in those days, his would have been filled with milk. McCool quit the Leafs after 22 games the following year and went home, claiming he was "sick and tired." One unnamed Leaf employee said the goalie left because he was "sick and tired of arguing with the team over a $500 pay raise."

He was replaced by Turk Broda, home from the war, and never returned to the NHL.

I can't wait to tell Howie and the boys about Frank "Ulcers" McCool.

A Final Word...

If you were a star in the NHL, at the peak of your career, would you turn down millions of dollars over the long term in favour of a one-year deal simply because it gives you a chance—just a chance—to see your name engraved on the Stanley Cup?

That's what winger Marian Hossa did in July, 2008.

Hossa, 29, shrugged off incredible riches offered by other clubs in order to sign a contract for a single season with Detroit. The Red Wings had defeated Hossa's former team, the Pittsburgh Penguins, in the 2008 finals and are favoured to win again in 2009.

Both Detroit general manager Ken Holland and Hossa's agent, Ritch Winter, were surprised by Hossa's decision.

"I told Ritch and Marian that I couldn't offer more than $7.4 million because that's what Nick Lidstrom earns," Holland said. "And it would have to be for one year. They had been asking for more, but in the end Marian made the decision. 'I'll take it,' he said. And he looked happy."

Winter, the lawyer who helped Carl Brewer and others bring down Al Eagleson years ago, simply shook his head. "I've never heard of a player taking $85 million less than he was offered by other clubs," said Winter. "It's never happened in hockey. It shows how much winning the Stanley Cup means to Marian."

Someday, perhaps, Hossa will have a tale to tell about the Stanley Cup. But if Bryan Trottier can take the Cup home to bed with him, if Clark Gillies can feed his dog from it, if Guy Lafleur can pilfer it from the trunk of a car, if Red Kelly's infant son can poop in it, if King Clancy can use it as a bill collector and holder of cigar butts, if it can be booted into a canal, left on a street corner, and hoisted to a mountaintop, Hossa will have to be creative if he hopes to add to the legendary stories.

First, he'll have to win it.